1

The Science of Introverts: Explore the Personality Spectrum for Self-Discovery, Self-Awareness, & Self-Care. Design a Life That Fits

By Peter Hollins,
Author and Researcher at
peterhollins.com

Table of Contents

The Science of Introverts: Explore the Personality Spectrum for Self-Discovery, Self-Awareness, & Self-Care. Learn to Design a Life That Suits You

Table of Contents

Introduction

My good friend named James told me a story about his childhood that resonated with me on a few levels. Supposedly, when he was a child, his fifth-grade teacher was trying to choose a class representative to send to the mock student government. Presumably, the student government at the elementary school was dealing with extremely important matters such as whether there should be one or two pizza days a month. These were high stakes, and James felt pressure to get in there and take care of business.

His teacher pulled three candidates to the front of the class, one of them being my friend. James is someone who could talk your ears off if he wanted, and the teacher positioned my friend on the right side while he positioned the quietest child on the left side. In the middle was someone who was neither extremely talkative nor extremely quiet.

The teacher began with putting his hand on my friend's shoulder and explained to the class, "You see, I can't have James represent us at the student government because he talks too much. Being in government, you have to be able to listen to others, and you can't take up all the talking time for yourself." Then he told James to sit down. Ouch.

I didn't ask him what happened to this teacher in later years, but we can safely assume that interacting with children was not his calling.

Next, the teacher walked to the quiet child and put his hand on his shoulder in the same way. "It's also a bad idea to send someone like Kenneth to the student government because he's so quiet you wouldn't know he was there. A government is all about representing a group of people, and that's impossible to do if you're a wallflower!" Then he told Kenneth to sit down. This was getting brutal. What was the teacher going to say about the middle child, Julia?

The teacher put his hand on Julia's shoulder and said, "Julia is exactly the type of person we should send to our student government. She isn't quiet but doesn't talk too much. She can do both, and in this world, you need to be able to listen and talk."

For all his clumsy and blunt delivery, the teacher was 100% correct about one thing. To function at our best among friends, meeting strangers, and in society, we must be able to bring a balance of listening and speaking. Too much speaking, and people will grow tired of listening to your monologues. Too much listening, and people will grow bored of launching their own monologue.

Of course, for our purposes, we are talking about the tendency of people to be introverted, extroverted, and somewhere in between. There exists a wealth of personality traits, yet one of the most widely discussed and fretted-over traits is simply how social someone is. This is even more so in recent years, when people seemingly take joy and pride in categorizing themselves in one way or the other. Perhaps the allure is similar to knowing which horoscope sign you are or how your blood type corresponds to your personality.

But unlike those two pursuits, how innately social we are has just a *little* bit more scientific grounding.

The scale of introversion to extroversion was devised by the famous psychologist Carl Jung in the 1920s in an attempt to quantify people. By quantifying people and identifying their temperaments, presumably they could capitalize on their strengths and buttress their weaknesses. While this sounds ideal, you probably know from your own experience that perception can change drastically as a result of a simple label—sometimes for better but often for worse.

Let's imagine the world as a party. In that party, introverts are clinging to the walls while extroverts are in the center of every room. People are a bit more nuanced than that and don't neatly fall into black and white dichotomies.

No matter how you identify or have been told you identify, let's draw back the curtain and begin the process of understanding the real differences and similarities inherent to your unique temperament. This is a wide-ranging book that draws on decades of psychological research about what makes people tick.

There are true physical and neurobiological differences; it turns out that you *are* wired differently than your friends who want to call it a night at 8:00 p.m. and those who aren't satisfied even at 3:00 a.m. And from those differences, there are some very real differences in the types of life that are preferred, sought out, and ultimately chosen. These lead to differences in happiness, careers, and even romantic relationships.

Introvert, extrovert, ambivert—where do you fall on the spectrum and what does it mean for you? Have you been searching for the wrong thing in your life all along? *The Science of Introverts* is in actuality the science of identity, personality, and who you are. Let's take the first step in (re)discovering yourself and gaining clarity on who you really are.

Chapter 1. The Personality Spectrum

I have always been labeled as an introvert. It's not a proud proclamation or confession; it's just reality. During childhood, I used to go straight home after school instead of staying at the playground to socialize with friends. When I was a teenager, I would spend my weekends alone in my room, playing the guitar or simply watching television by myself. It wasn't because I didn't have friends to hang out with. I just seemed to have a better time by myself, especially after long days of being around other people. This pattern continued well into adulthood.

Because of this, I have heard the word "introvert" used to describe me roughly one million times. The first few times, I shrugged it off and ignored it. But then I got to wondering what people really meant by it and if I should be worried. What is an introvert, *really*? That's an answer that requires some background information.

Introversion is one of the major personality traits studied in many psychological theories. The word *introvert* was used for the very first time, along with the word *extrovert*, during the 1920s when renowned psychologist Carl Jung published *Psychologische Typen* (or *Psychological Types*, as it's known in English). It was further developed and refined by Hans Eysenck, and it entered mainstream lexicon with Isabel Meyers and Katharine Briggs in 1943 when it became a part of the MBTI—Meyers-Briggs Type Indicator, a test for helping people find careers well suited for their individual personalities.

Today, the introvert-extrovert typology is even more relevant. According to Jung, introversion is a psychological mode wherein an individual considers his or her inner reality of utmost importance. If you've done much reading on this topic, this first chapter might be somewhat of a review and confirmation for you.

This means introverts tend to be more inward-focused, and they often retreat from the outside world to be able to focus their energy inwards. Extroversion, on the other hand, pushes people to be more outgoing and to rely on external sources (people, circumstances, and environment) for stimulation. The differences between the two personality types boil down to how these individuals allocate their energy. While extroverts find social interactions energizing, introverts find this activity draining, so they avoid it as much as they can. This simple difference creates a domino effect of differing lifestyles and preferences.

Introverts are people who tend to be more focused on their internal thoughts and emotions rather than being engrossed in trying to find stimulation from the external environment. These individuals normally keep things to themselves and are defensive of the demands of the outside world. They are contemplative, cautious, and similar to a cat—sometimes the cat wants to play, and other times you can't get them out from their hiding spot under the bed.

In reality, extroversion and introversion exist on a continuum—there are people who fall on the far ends of the spectrum as well as people in between who exhibit tendencies from both sides.

How do we know if a person is an introvert? There are a number of traits introverts possess that can distinguish them.

For one, introverts don't mind being alone—often, they prefer it. But it's not because they hate people. Don't confuse it with social anxiety or even shyness. They are just easily exhausted by social interaction, which includes simply talking to another person or being in public. They are comfortable spending time by themselves and see it as a reprieve from the noisy world outside. Many people find this trait undesirable because Western society holds an internalized extrovert ideal, meaning they have higher regard for people who invest more time socializing than those who prefer not to.

For a better understanding, we can view introversion and extroversion by looking at an imaginary social battery.

For the introvert, their battery drains quickly when they are in a setting that demands a lot of interaction. Their social battery regains power only when they spend adequate time without the company of others, in the confines of their private space, and doing things that require no contact with the outside world.

For example, an introvert who spent an entire night at a social gathering is more likely to isolate himself from people the following day. This person cannot handle so many interactions, so they need to retreat to the comfort of solitude. Sometimes it takes hours or even days for them to recharge their battery and prepare themselves for another social affair, depending on how introverted they are and how intense the interaction was.

They can easily entertain themselves by reading a book, watching a movie, or killing time with one-player games. Introverts also find small talk a waste of time and energy. It exhausts their social battery faster than any other activity, and it seems to be all for nothing. Because of this, introverts are more likely to participate in purposeful conversations that have a clear direction. If they are going to expend their precious social energy, it may as well be for something that is significant or intimate. Nothing comes without a cost.

They like the *idea* of parties, family gatherings, and a night out with friends. However, participating in these events is a real chore for them. Sometimes they need a lot of convincing to say yes, and it could be difficult for them to gather the energy needed to socialize on days where all they want to do is have a relaxing soak in the bathtub.

Anticipation can be exciting, yet actual engagement is more typically exhausting. For them, an ideal weekend night is as simple as having to stay at home, enjoying a movie marathon, and eating a bag of popcorn. If you are interacting with someone who appears to be antisocial or unapproachable, it's possible they are merely introverted with a social battery that's fully drained at the moment.

For an introvert, an ideal party is one that is quiet, keeps people busy with their own business, has an agenda, and has a set ending time—and yet people still might leave early. You probably wouldn't even call it a party because it would involve people spending time together but not necessarily engaging with each other. A book club is a good example of this. They are more comfortable when they are familiar with how the program goes and when it will end, because that way they can pace themselves and their social batteries.

You might be able to guess that the extrovert's social battery functions in the exact opposite way—charging up in the presence of others and slowly draining when spending time alone. If the introvert is a hiding cat, the extrovert is a golden retriever who wants to play fetch all the time.

Introverts can appear fickle or complicated in the eyes of everyone else. It's important for the friends of introverts to gain an understanding of their nature so they don't take things personally when their attempts at socialization are rejected. Again, you just might be dealing with someone who needs to pay attention to their waning social battery.

Introversion is not always so obvious, especially to introverts. Some people don't even realize what they are seeking until they have behavior patterns pointed out to them, such as an aversion to large group settings or a tendency to leave events early. While introverts make up a large portion of the population, one which seems to increase every day, there are still misconceptions about this personality type.

As mentioned previously, introverts are automatically categorized as shy and anxious people. They might also be seen as rude or unapproachable.

This association is understandable, since it cannot be denied that many introverts do possess these traits. However, it is not true that all introverts are nervous, antisocial wrecks. Not all of them are timid and quiet. Being shy and anxious can accompany introversion, but it does not define it. With a charged social battery, an introvert is indistinguishable from an extrovert—it's what they do afterward, when they are tired, that differentiates them. If you see someone who appears to be shy or unapproachable, chances are they are simply socially tapped out.

Another misconception about introverts is that you can tell one based solely on observing them. A person's activity alone is not an accurate indicator of whether he or she is an introvert.

For instance, a party animal is not necessarily an extrovert. Being a loner most of the time does not make you an introvert. A person's activity might just be indicative that they are constantly living life outside of their comfort zones. The person you always see alone may not be necessarily an introvert; she might be forced into that situation.

It could be that the task is a requirement of her job, but the truth is that she is physically, emotionally, and psychologically exhausted from all the meetups. People are adaptable and will rise to the occasion when necessary, but in the end, this leads to many unrealized introverts trying to put on a poor impression of an extrovert for years and years.

You might think you're weird or that something is wrong with you if you hate going to bars while all your friends love it— you just have a different personality than them. Remember, it's what people prefer to do to relax and unwind that determines where they fall on the spectrum.

Introverts don't need to be babied, but it's important to keep a few things in mind so *you* don't get your feelings hurt around them.

- Respect their need for alone time and don't take it personally.
- Allow them to adapt and interact at their own pace, because chances are that they are already uncomfortable just by being there.
- Don't jump to apathy or malice when a depleted social battery could be an explanation.

We meet introverts every day, and we have to learn how to create more harmonious relationships with them. If you identify as an introvert, understanding yourself better will help you connect and coexist with others. Acknowledging the fact that we are not all similar helps create a balance and also frees you from unfair expectations you may feel from society at large.

Being an introvert is not a bad thing. If you love chocolate, can you judge someone for loving vanilla instead? Introverts of the world unite (separately, for only a limited amount of time, and without having to commit ahead of time)!

The Extrovert Ideal

What do you want to do when you're tired? Do you want to spend time with friends or lock yourself in a room?

Understanding your answer to this question is essential to becoming more self-aware. We've talked about how introverts must seclude themselves for energy, and now we turn our attention to the extrovert who uses other people as energy sources. What characterizes the extrovert?

The most extroverted among us are those who simply can't get enough of being with and around other people. When they are by themselves, extroverts may feel bored, restless, anxious, or tired as their energy levels deplete from the lack of social stimulation. They are like flowers wilting without adequate sunlight and water.

It is a natural tendency for people to enjoy the things at which they are naturally skilled, so it may not surprise you to learn that extroverts are often the leaders of the pack when it comes to socializing. It is not by accident that extroverts will often find themselves at the center of attention while at social gatherings—that is where they often feel most in their element, and they have had plenty of practice.

When you picture someone excelling in a social situation, you are picturing the stereotype of the extrovert. This ranges from partygoers to salesmen who can talk to anyone and people who arrange parties on a weekly basis. They are seen as the hub of socialization, and thus, people want to be around them as well.

This conceptualization is known as the *extrovert ideal*, where, at least in Western cultures, extroverts are seen to be preferred and more likable (Susan Cain). It can certainly seem that way from first glance, as having someone around who likes being around is usually a good thing. Being able to energetically perform and thrive in the spotlight certainly garners more attention than not.

One important caveat here is that, just like all introverts are not necessarily anxious or shy, though some are, all extroverts are not necessarily charming or likable. Surely you can picture an acquaintance who enjoys being around people, but the feeling is not mutual. They lack self-awareness and don't realize people are trying to avoid rather than engage them.

Extroversion by itself isn't a positive trait, despite what most media will tell you; it's just a description of what people like to do in their most natural state, which so happens to create more interaction than other people. It's a trait that happens to demand attention and create presence. After all, just because people love baseball doesn't mean they excel at it. Being an extrovert is not better than being an introvert, and vice versa. Our society needs both types of people to function correctly.

While their communication skills are valued and envied, they are sometimes accompanied by another pitfall—*distractibility*. This is especially so in the workplace. There are elements of the inability to delay gratification and seeking dopamine-inducing interaction immediately.

The tendency of the extrovert to always focus on people can make them less efficient and productive. They may know that there's a big stack of papers waiting to be read on their desk, but the faint sounds of a lively conversation going on in the break room down the hall are just too tempting not to go investigate. Moreover, they just might grow exhausted at the prospect of grinding through paperwork alone. If productivity and the ability to get things done is a product of solitude and alone time, then you might say they're at a disadvantage in many careers, feeling especially drained at the prospect of late nights with documents.

What might the ideal daily schedule look like for somebody who is highly extroverted?

At a minimum, they would likely prefer to enjoy each of their meals in the company of others. Colleagues from work, friends, family, you name it—as long as they get to frequently spend time with other people, an extrovert will feel more energized throughout the day. Even if they are totally swamped with work and only have 15 minutes to eat lunch, that time would be better spent eating in the crowded cafeteria than being confined in their office or cubicle. It would be like a shot of espresso in itself.

Alone time can still be enjoyable to extroverts when they are being entertained, even if they aren't reenergized by the solitude. Entertainment is entertainment, after all. But without entertainment, solitude is not generally desirable.

Extroverts think less about their inner feelings than introverts and are more focused on their environments, so any prolonged period spent alone with a lack of stimulation can quickly result in feelings of anxiousness or boredom.

When it's time to blow off steam after a long week, extroverts will typically seek out a night full of social interaction—the more, the better.

I witnessed this firsthand when I went out one night with my highly extroverted friend Katie. Within mere minutes of walking into a bar, she managed to integrate herself into a group of six complete strangers, making interesting small talk and garnering the group's full attention. Katie was more energetic than she'd been all week, and so we hopped from one bar to the next, meeting more and more people as the night wore on into the early hours of the morning.

She was like a vampire, gaining energy from the faltering introvert—me. I can only wonder how long Katie could have kept her socializing up, as she was still going at full-steam when the last call sounded and the bars began to empty out.

Whether they are basking in the attention of their closest friends or just sitting in a café alone with people and commotion all around them, the important thing is that they are in the presence of other people, because that is what energizes them. Sponge or vampire, you get the idea.

As you are learning more about the personality types, it is natural that you may begin categorizing your friends and family based on the experiences you've had with them. When you do this, it's important to understand that there are plenty of misconceptions about extroverts as well: for instance, all extroverts are charming, likable, and have limitless friends. Katie illustrates one of them quite well.

For all of the new people she interacted with that night, Katie didn't get the contact information for a single one. This was surprising to me as I was observing it, because in many instances she seemed to genuinely connect with the people she was meeting.

With each passing positive interaction, I began to realize that it was *the social interaction itself* that brought value to Katie, not the potential to make friends. She moved between groups like a butterfly but seemed to stay only on shallow topics and cracking jokes. When I thought about it, I rarely engaged her on anything deeper than how our days went and we rarely connected on personal topics.

You see, we often see extroverts interacting with a high volume of people and think or assume that they must, therefore, have a high volume of friends. This isn't necessarily true. In fact, it has been scientifically proven through studies related to Dunbar's number by Professor Robin Dunbar of Oxford University that the average number of close friends anyone can truly have hovers around five people. (*Dunbar's number*, by the way, is the proposal that humans can only really know and care about 150 people at a time.)

What extroverts tend to have is a lot of *acquaintances*—people they know and interact with on occasion, or even on a consistent basis, but aren't close friends with. Social media further contributes to the misconception that extroverts have tons of friends, as the sheer volume of acquaintances will often correlate to more Instagram followers and Facebook friends—the modern measures of popularity in our digital, interconnected world.

This leads us to another misconception about extroverts, and it's one that can be particularly harmful in your relationships with them.

Interacting with extroverts can easily leave you with the impression that they are always in a good mood and social. It's common for extroverts to have bubbly personalities, which can be interpreted as them always feeling happy and not falling victim to negative emotions to the same extent as less extroverted people.

Not only is this false, but it can cause you to subconsciously develop unreasonable expectations for the extroverts you interact with to always be energetic and positive. Individuals with extroverted tendencies are subject to moods, blues, phases, and times of introspection as well, and you should be supportive of them in these times just as you would with your quieter and less socially active friends.

You may also believe that most extroverts prefer shallow small talk or are even incapable of the same levels of deep thought that a quiet and less social person may experience. Extroverts can be deep thinkers too, and they can certainly be excellent conversational partners on intellectual subjects because of their innate ability to communicate well.

One aspect in particular that changes as you move across the social temperament spectrum is how individuals work through their problems.

Extroverts are fully capable of introspection and may handle some matters privately. But remember, they are more accustomed to taking cues from the external world. They may default to discussing their personal problems with a trusted friend or family member. It's not that they need the guidance; they just function better outside their own heads.

So the next time you're stuck on the phone with your extroverted friend who just keeps going on and on about whatever is distressing them without stopping to hear your opinion, don't take it as a slight. You are providing a valuable service to your friend, as just having somebody to talk through their thoughts with can be extremely helpful for extroverts when they find themselves in a predicament.

Extroverts have dealt with these types of frustrating misconceptions for most of their lives, so they are sure to appreciate when you make the effort to understand them better before jumping to conclusions about their personalities and preferences.

As you read onward through this book, these are the fundamental ideas about extroverts that you should keep in the back of your mind:

- Extroverts enjoy being around people because this is how they get energy. This doesn't always translate beyond mere chatter, activity, and motion.
- Extroverts are capable of everything an introvert is, just not all of it, all the time.

Being able to quickly identify where somebody lies on the extrovert and introvert spectrum can provide immense benefits if you understand how to use that information.

When you are interacting with extroverts, be mindful that they are feeding off of your energy, not trapped inside of their own thoughts. They're not trying to invade your space or pry into your life; they're just enjoying being in your company. Whether you enjoy listening and learning about others, or just need somebody to talk to about what's going on in your life, an extroverted friend will likely enjoy the interaction with you.

Moreover, understanding where you lie on the spectrum and how that influences your personality and decision-making is the first step toward learning how to make the changes you want in your life.

If you are extroverted, chances are that sitting in a cubicle and keeping to yourself all day will make you miserable. Pursue work and hobbies that provide you with plenty of opportunities for interaction throughout the day and keep you enjoying the present moment. As for introverts, having more extroverted influences in your life may make for more enjoyable experiences when you socialize, and you may even learn a thing or two about effective ways to communicate and connect with other people. You might also stop inviting people over to your home or at least set times for kicking people out.

We've given an overview of the two ends of the spectrum of personality, but to assume that everyone must fit into one of these definitions is a false dichotomy. Indeed, you might feel that what you've read thus far is inaccurate or blurry. It's true that it doesn't accurately reflect what most people in the world truly are. The next section, however, does.

What Lies Between

Hans Eysenck was the first to coin the term *ambivert* to define a person as one who manifests the characteristics of both an introvert and an extrovert.

They are in the proverbial middle, though there is no exact point for *middle* and it's impossible to achieve the exact *middle* between one personality type and the other. With something as dynamic as temperament and personality traits, the pendulums keep swinging from one side to the other. Just because we throw a temper tantrum one day doesn't mean we can't be calm and collected the next.

As a reminder, to the introvert, the *real* world is an inner world of ideas, thoughts, and perception generated by their own minds. An extrovert is one who derives energy from the outside world, other people, and things that exist within that person's environment.

And yet Carl Jung himself, the man who coined those two personality types, didn't think a pure introvert or extrovert existed. He said, "There is no such thing as a pure introvert or extrovert... Such a person would be in the lunatic asylum!" The ambivert is a representation of the vast middle ground between a pure introvert and pure extrovert. Just like without positive and negative emotions, we can't realistically function without both sides of the spectrum. For every yin there is a yang, and so on and so forth.

There are numerous biological factors that differentiate personality types, but the vast majority of people are permeable enough to move from being more or less introverted to being more or less extroverted, depending upon the situation, our motivations, and the people we are surrounded by.

Writer Jonathan Alexander states, "We all have a little bit of introvert and a little bit of extrovert in us, no matter which personality we display the most." Everyone has these mood swings. They are natural, provided they are not extreme and unstable. You simply wouldn't react the same way if you were coming from a funeral versus coming from a party.

Sometimes an introvert may be the person never wanting the party to stop and having a seemingly endless supply of social energy. This would seem to be at odds with the modus operandi of the introvert, until you learn they are trying to impress someone, like a potential romantic interest or their boss.

Though the introvert might prefer more solitude, there are situations in which they will rise to the occasion and act outside their character and comfort zone. And what about the extrovert? Sometimes you might see them leave a social gathering early, or they might appear to be a wallflower, stuck to the wall far away from other people. This would also be uncharacteristic of them, but you might learn they have just gotten released from their job or are newly single after a rough breakup.

People have dashes of both the introverted style and the extroverted style, depending on everything else going on in their lives. Your social battery, tolerance for people, and interest in others depends a great deal upon the context in which you are doing that (at work, for instance) or upon your feelings and general mood (as may occur if you have to weather a severe storm in order to get to a lecture on time). That's why you can't tell someone's disposition simply by looking at their actions.

No one is exactly the same every day. For weeks, you may be preoccupied by a presentation you have to make to the board of directors, and you might be introverted.

You might want some "quiet time" in your office to prepare for your leadership event. Suppose you don't have the luxury of spending time alone at your workstation and reflecting.

You may then realize that it is necessary to relate to your coworkers, whether you want to or not. Of course, you want to avoid coming across as distracted, so you may enter a phase of extroversion to compensate for what looks like reckless mind-wandering. In the interest of balance, you discover that you can operate quite well with interchanges between yourself and your colleagues. It's a good thing and means you have the ability to adapt to different circumstances like a chameleon. With time, we can build a certain amount of tolerance to it, but that doesn't mean it's not still outside of our comfort zones.

The world is not black and white and made up of solely hermits and partygoers. In truth, most introverts would become quite anxious if they were isolated for long periods. They might even develop "cabin fever." Likewise, most extroverts would feel their anxiety level rise if they had to attend one social event after another without enjoying some time to themselves.

For example, let's say that a human resources manager at a manufacturing plant receives a complaint from a regular client who was having difficulty with a piece of equipment they bought from the plant. It would be the human resource person's job to remedy the problem. So he would have to have the engineer contact the client about the problem.

By stereotype, engineers tend to be somewhat introverted and tend to steer away from customer contact. Engineers are also stereotypically a tad irascible and find it frustrating when customers don't follow the written instructions. In private, engineers sometimes even say, "Customers are *stupid!*" Of course, no one wants a customer to receive a call from the manufacturer and be called *"stupid!"*

It is vital that introverts be able to shift focus and become extroverted to suit the situation. In addition, they must bring control and patience into the dialogue. Those are the ideal candidates for corporate positions.

During the introvert/extrovert encounter, the engineer needs to move away from his introverted role and patiently explain the issue to the client in a nonthreatening manner.

If you pigeon-hole yourself into being an introvert and consider yourself always as such, it can become a self-fulfilling prophecy. You may limit yourself to a life of isolation and essentially live inside yourself. You'll do away with connecting with people and attempt to rely only on yourself. Worst of all, you'll limit your potential. No great leader's autobiography ever said, "I did it all myself."

On the other hand, if you determine that you are exclusively an extrovert, you may restrict yourself and fail to open up your mind to educational possibilities that can advance your career and make more money for yourself and your family. Essentially, you might find yourself distracted and caught up in the moment instead of planning and engaging in periods of deep work. This unfortunately happens to students who go to college and spend most of their nights partying. Most of us have seen that happen.

Having a combination of introverted and extroverted traits make us more capable and adaptable in anything we want to do. It is what composes the various careers we undertake. Without adventurers, we wouldn't explore the world. Without writers, our minds would not be enlightened. This happy variety makes life worth living—and allows you to live it to the fullest. It also produces challenges that help us grow and reach our full potential.

Ninety-nine percent of people are ambiverts. From a person who is predominantly introverted, we expect at least some extroverted behaviors;

otherwise, we feel like we are talking to a robot. From a person who is predominantly extroverted, we occasionally expect silence and sedate behaviors; otherwise, we feel like we are talking to someone who won't remember our name later.

Ultimately, it's about moderation and balance. We are all capable of showing a wide range of emotions. We would quickly lose heart if our lives were always spent in cavorting with friends or secluded in the solitude of our dark rooms. Life calls us to both action and thought. A band that just plays one note merits no applause.

Society needs us to be dynamic in order to evolve. Just like the popular labels of introvert, extrovert, and ambivert, people have started classifying themselves as *extroverted introverts* and *introverted extroverts*.

An extroverted introvert derives energy from being alone yet participates in social activities and enjoys them, for the most part. Like a cellphone, the extroverted introvert needs time to "recharge." After that, and only after that, is accomplished can extroverted introverts live their lives in a fruitful and natural way.

An introverted extrovert derives energy through social interaction. After exploring the vistas of other people's experiences, the introverted extrovert needs time to reclaim his individuality and uniqueness. That is the time they solidify the elements within themselves that are beautiful and meaningful. That is the time they establish an identity that makes them distinct— different from all others they know.

These are all different ways to define ambivert. They are just different names for the exact same thing.

Remember that the traditional introvert/extrovert scale is a false dichotomy. People may lean one way or the other, but all that really means is that they are still somewhere in the middle. That is the way it is supposed to be. Despite the labels or categories, we are more similar to each other than we like to readily admit.

We won't benefit from living up to our own expectations instead of exploring and destroying them. To stubbornly adhere to a label or side of the spectrum is also to deny the true complexity of our human nature. It is that which makes us real, three-dimensional beings.

Introvert or Highly Sensitive?

A final piece of the temperament spectrum is to distinguish between introverts and similar labels.

The general perception of introverts—most usually coming from non-introverts—is that in addition to having different social leanings and insights, they're *really, really sensitive*.

That may be true to a certain extent. The way introverts deal with the world at least implies that they're more emotionally responsive to certain sensory stimuli. But there are important differences between introverts and what are known as *highly sensitive people*, or HSPs for short. Psychologists Elaine Aron and Arthur Aron coined the term HSP in the 1990s. They found that HSPs make up roughly 15–20% of the general population, so they are not as rare or misunderstood as they may sometimes feel. While introverts and HSPs have some things in common, it's important to draw a distinction so you can understand yourself better.

HSPs are viewed differently according to who's doing the viewing. Those who are more inclined to be intuitive (and diplomatic) might call HSPs "empaths," people who have an almost otherworldly ability to understand someone else's mental or emotional being. Those who are clinical professionals might say HSPs possess "sensory processing sympathy," which amounts to an extremely sensitive central nervous system and a strong response to various stimuli. And people who are *in*sensitive would call HSPs "too darned sensitive."

How do you detect if someone's a highly sensitive person? Remember that like being an introvert, sensitivity is a *quality*, a personal characteristic. It is not a character flaw, nor is it a terrific asset. It's simply something someone is. You either have a lot of it, not enough of it, or just the right amount.

HSPs tend to get overly affected by excessive outside stimuli. They may get overwhelmed out by extremely bright lights or loud noises. They may be overly affected by a sentimental song or a tear-jerking movie. HSPs *do* have a stronger response to negative experiences. They feel profound impact when they feel slighted or hurt. HSPs are also susceptible to being greatly offended by people who sincerely have no intent to hurt or criticize them.

When it comes to downtime, HSPs don't just like it—they desperately need to have it. After they've spent a hectic day in a thriving, overactive, and possibly threatening world, HSPs absolutely need a prescribed amount of time to relax and recover. The same researchers who coined the term went on to elaborate that HSPs are characterized by DOES—an acronym that describes four of the main traits of the HSP.

D stands for *depth of processing*. HSPs do not simply hear something—they hear it, analyze it, ruminate on it, and file it away for later. In this way, everything becomes interconnected in a web of thoughts and processing. This makes the subtlest stimuli grow in size, sometimes to unreasonable heights. Research by professor Jadzia Jagiellowicz has confirmed that there is extra activity in the parts of the brain of an HSP when put to tasks of analysis and observation.

O stands for *overstimulation*. This is where the comparison to introverts may primarily come from. HSPs are more prone to feeling overwhelmed by their environments, including the people around them. Naturally, this causes them to want to retreat to solitude. In addition, if everything in an environment appears to hold significance and meaning through deep processing, then it can be difficult to understand what to focus on.

E stands for *emotional reactivity*. What does this mean? It means that HSPs are more easily triggered into negative or positive emotional states. A single movie can cause tears of terror, happiness, sadness, or anger. For this reason, E also stands for *empathy*—feeling the emotions of other people and assuming them as your own. This is partially because the mirror neurons of the HSP—neurons that put us into the perspective of whatever we are observing—are particularly active.

S is for *sensing the subtle*. Something is never nothing; something always has to be *something*. This means that even in a blank room, an HSP may find something to question or analyze. There is always significance that can be teased out; the radar is always functioning at high alert. Obviously, this can be tiring, especially when the subtle truly turns out to be nothing.

This isn't necessarily about having great vision or powerful hearing aids—it's about perceiving complexity in all areas of life. Taken together with the other elements of

DOES, you can see how the HSP can feel paralyzed and simply want to spend time alone—something they share with introverts.

Introverts and HSPs do share some rather identifiable similarities. Both types deal with heightened sensitivities. Both of them have neural bases for their "conditions." Both tend to be more cautious, and both place a high value on "me time."

However, there are a few major ways in which introverts and HSPs contrast. Not all HSPs are introverts. Studies have seen that three out of 10 highly sensitive people actually lean toward *extroversion*. They process emotions with great complexity and have to recharge themselves after extensive overstimulation—but they also feed off the energy of social contact and consort with a lot of other people. Introverts do the reverse: they *discharge* energy in social situations. Long exposure to them eventually wears them out and they have to recharge.

HSPs are not identified by the expense or collection of social energy, however. Their state doesn't have anything to do with the increase or decrease of dopamine and other neurotransmitters, the brain's pleasure and reward regulator, and what roughly defines introverts and extroverts.

Rather, HSPs are defined by their special response to stimuli and the deep processing of emotions. So why are HSPs so sensitive? It's all about their central nervous systems.

Human beings function best when their nervous systems are aroused and aware at a reasonable level. If their nervous systems aren't sufficiently engaged, then they get bored and potentially depressed. If their nervous systems are too stimulated, they get stressed out, awkward, clumsy, and basically turn into an overwhelmed mess.

HSPs' central nervous systems are wired like a time bomb. They get overstimulated and aroused a lot more quickly than other people—even non-HSP introverts. This is what defines them. The more information they have to process, the closer that bomb is to exploding. That's why they have deep emotional responses to tear-jerking movies that more hardened people would call too hokey or sappy.

There are two different kinds of mental "systems" that regulate how a person responds to a stimulus: "behavioral activation" and "behavioral inhibition." When someone with behavioral activation tendencies receives information from sensory inputs, their brain orders them to move. Stimuli activate behavior. Someone with more pronounced behavior inhibition receives that same sensory information but orders the body to move *away*. Stimuli inhibit behavior.

HSPs are strong in behavioral inhibition—they seek to avoid mental overstimulation.

I'm worried that I might have painted a picture of HSPs as constantly on edge and liable to detonate at any moment. That's not entirely fair, at least in the suggestion that HSPs take away from others' energies rather than give back to it. Remember, sensitivity isn't a defect—it's simply a trait.

Even with HSPs, what really matters more is what they *do* with their sensitivity.

They care very strongly about other people's feelings and can channel those deep feelings into great works of charity or assistance. They have no hesitation in expressing great gratitude for what they have. They can also enjoy events, food, entertainment, and other simple pleasures on a level that other people simply can't. True, they carry a lot of their past emotions with them—they tend to keep the memory of past failures around for much longer than most other people do—but that ongoing processing of their emotions means they may be able to help other less cognizant people process *their* emotions.

You might be wondering at this point whether you qualify as a highly sensitive person. You'll be happy to know there's a heavily circulated "test" that purports to give you the answer.

This test contains 23 statements that you can label as "true" or "false" as they pertain to your feelings. If you feel you strongly or somewhat agree with the statement, you'd mark it "true." If you strongly or somewhat disagree, you'd mark it false. Here you go:

- I seem to be aware of subtleties in my environment.

- Other people's moods affect me.

- I tend to be very sensitive to pain.

- I find myself needing to withdraw during busy days, into bed or into a darkened room or any place where I can have some privacy and relief from stimulation.

- I am particularly sensitive to the effects of caffeine.

- I am easily overwhelmed by things like bright lights, strong smells, coarse fabrics, or sirens close by.

- I have a rich, complex inner life.

- I am made uncomfortable by loud noises.

- I am deeply moved by the arts or music.

- I am conscientious.

- I startle easily.

- I get rattled when I have a lot to do in a short amount of time.

- When people are uncomfortable in a physical environment, I tend to know what needs to be done to make it more comfortable (like changing the lighting or the seating).

- I am annoyed when people try to get me to do too many things at once.

- I try hard to avoid making mistakes or forgetting things.

- I make it a point to avoid violent movies and TV shows.

- I become unpleasantly aroused when a lot is going on around me.

- Being very hungry creates a strong reaction in me, disrupting my concentration or mood.

- Changes in my life shake me up.

- I notice and enjoy delicate or fine scents, tastes, sounds, and works of art.

- I make it a high priority to arrange my life to avoid upsetting or overwhelming situations.

- When I must compete or be observed while performing a task, I become so nervous or shaky that I do much worse than I would otherwise.

- When I was a child, my parents or teachers seemed to see me as sensitive or shy.

If you've answered "true" to at least 12 of these statements—slightly more than half—then you, too, are probably an HSP. Remember that sensitivity, even a surplus of it, isn't an inherent fault. It's a trait; it's simply the way you are. What matters is how you use your sensitivity for constructive purposes. It may be a challenge, but it's loaded with the potential for good.

Takeaways:

- The personality spectrum has been defined in many ways throughout history, but people have increasingly gravitated toward classifying themselves in terms of their capacity for social interaction and how important a person's internal or external world was. It was later refined to understand that introverts are depleted by social interaction, while extroverts are recharged by it. This leads to opposite types of lifestyles, as you might suspect. There are a variety of misunderstandings associated with these labels, but keep in mind that this scale solely judges what makes people feel recharged—solitude or company.

- Even though Carl Jung defined these two terms and forever created a spectrum, he recognized that it was impossible for people to not be in the middle. These are called ambiverts, and the vast majority of us are ambiverts. We act according to social obligation, circumstance, and duty, which means you can't necessarily tell someone's temperament just by their actions alone. We might skew to one side or another and can further categorize ourselves with terms like extroverted introvert or introverted extrovert. This still means we are in the middle in terms of our social battery, capacity, and desire.

- A point of distinction must be made between introverts and highly sensitive people—HSPs. They may appear identical at first glance, but that's where the similarities end. The HSP is characterized by the acronym DOES, which stands for depth of processing, overstimulation, emotional reactivity, and sensing the subtle. This all amounts to HSPs wearing a proverbial hearing aid turned up to the max when none is needed. They are *sensitive*, and this merely overlaps with social capacity and recharging.

Chapter 2. Inside-Out

Despite the fact that we are all ambiverts first and foremost, the truth is that there are a few real biological differences between those who skew more one way than the other. Nature and nurture both have a part to play here.

If you have to psych yourself up for a big party or networking event, you can do that and act the part for as long as you need, but you'll probably be exhausted for the next day and a half. We might call this regressing to the mean or compensating for extreme exertion. Try as we might, sometimes we just can't change how we're biologically wired.

While factors including self-confidence, comfort with your social group, and health can all play roles in how you feel as a result of interactions with the people in your life, whether or not these interactions are a source of energy for you or a tax on it is largely predetermined by your brain structure. In this chapter, we explore all the biological bases for differences in this aspect of personality.

The differences generally have to do with how the brain perceives stimulation and then how it handles it. Our first stop is the prefrontal cortex.

The Prefrontal Cortex

The first major biological difference lies within the prefrontal cortex, which is generally the location for higher-level thinking and analysis. In 2012, Harvard psychologist Randy Buckner conducted a study that goes a long way in explaining how introverted or extroverted we might be.

Buckner and his team found that subjects of the study who identified as introverts had thicker gray matter in certain areas of the prefrontal cortex, while those who identified as extroverted tended to have thinner gray matter in those same prefrontal areas.

To lend some context, the prefrontal cortex is the area of the brain responsible for functions like abstract thought, planning, decision-making, attention span, and focus. If you are using logic or critical thinking, that's where it occurs. Thicker brain matter, meanwhile, is directly correlated with greater brainpower and cognitive ability with regard to all of those functions. You might feel a slight twinge of superiority from this knowledge, but it certainly doesn't allow us to draw the conclusion that introverts are smarter or more intelligent.

The only conclusion we can draw is that introverts naturally have higher-density brain matter in the area of the brain associated with typical introverted behaviors. In other words, the prefrontal cortex of introverts is more developed in exactly the way you would expect— introverts emphasize planning, analysis, focus, and introspection, and therefore, they have developed greater brain mass suited for that. It's not without its negatives, as these inhibit things like spontaneity, letting go of stress, and generally being more carefree.

Buckner's findings act to reinforce many of the stereotypes we hold about each of these personalities.

You've probably heard the phrase "live in the moment" or one of its variations throughout your life. We've accepted this as something to strive for and an important part of being happy and living life to the fullest. It means you are being brave and not letting yourself be held back by others or yourself. As it turns out, your propensity to "live in the moment" may be correlated with how you recharge your social energy and the corresponding density of brain matter in your prefrontal cortex.

Introverts, meanwhile, may often struggle to live up to this societal ideal. Because of their denser prefrontal cortexes, introverts dedicate more mental resources to abstract pondering, planning, and decision-making, all activities that are decidedly absent from the idea of seizing the day.

This reinforces Jung's proposal that introverts feel that the real world exists in their head. Accordingly, this also reinforces Jung's proposal that extroverts feel that the real world is what their environments show them.

As they don't dedicate as many neural resources to analyzing and decision-making, extroverts are able to respond more to their environments and simply react without thinking. They find it much easier to live in the moment, as their brains predisposition them to react to their environment as opposed to analyze, plan, focus, and ruminate as the introvert brain structure does.

Being spontaneous is something that simply happens naturally, rather than intentionally. It's not to say that extroverts don't think about consequences or are careless in making decisions; they just aren't innately wired to pause, think, and analyze first.

The increased prefrontal cortex of introverts also explains why they grow socially fatigued more quickly—because there is always cognitive work occurring in response to stimuli. A party is not just a party; a party is an analysis of the people, environment, conversations, and an endless chain of decisions to consider. It is endless observation and rumination on everything that is in the immediate environment. The classic journalistic questions (who, what, when, where, and especially *why*) are also in play.

Where the extrovert might take something at face value, the introvert can't help but deconstruct it.

This finding may help us to explain the role alcohol can play for introverts who drink. Alcohol is often referred to as a social lubricant, partially because it weakens inhibitions, decision-making, and critical analysis skills (Kenneth Abernathy, 2010).

Indeed, after numerous behavioral research studies in which scientists scanned people's brains as they consumed alcohol, it is now widely accepted that alcohol is directly responsible for reducing neural activity in the prefrontal cortex. Alcohol can temporarily cause people to be more in tune with their environments and less in their own heads, essentially behaving and feeling more extroverted than they typically are. We have a clear picture of what a drunk person looks and acts like. Some people say that alcohol frees you to act like the person you've always wanted to be, but most commonly, alcohol causes introverts to act more like extroverts!

Alcohol is not just used by people who need or want to be looser in their social interactions. Even individuals who are already highly extroverted may still enjoy alcohol, chiefly because they get to enjoy the presence of others and living in the moment to an even greater extent than usual—yet another example where, for many extroverts, more is better.

For those introverts who are searching for an escape from the feeling of being trapped inside their own heads as they analyze and introspect, unable to live in the moment, meditation can also achieve similar results to alcohol.

Specifically, meditation has been shown to weaken connections between the amygdala—the part of your brain responsible for your emotions—and the prefrontal cortex (Joshua Grant). This gives you greater control over your thoughts because they are less tied to your emotional states. Imagine that you are stuck in your head using the illustration of a hamster frantically running on his wheel.

This allows you to relax and approach your thoughts —actually, to *separate* yourself from your thoughts, function better, and prevent yourself from getting stuck in your head.

So because of different brain structures, introverts end up more in their heads. The second argument to support the biological basis of introverts living more in their heads than in their external environments comes from a study conducted in 2013 by Richard A. Depue and Yu Fu at Cornell University.

Researchers gathered 70 young males—a mix of introverts and extroverts, according to a standard personality test—and then split them into two random groups. The first group took the substance methylphenidate (MP)—also known as Ritalin—a central nervous system stimulant typically used to treat attention deficit hyperactive disorder (ADHD) and narcolepsy by increasing the production of dopamine and norepinephrine in the brain. The second group served as the experimental control and was given a placebo.

Both groups were shown a series of videos in a laboratory environment. They received either the Ritalin or the placebo for the first three days, and then on the fourth day, no drugs were administered.

Over the course of the study, researchers measured how strongly the participants associated the videos with the environment by testing subconscious traits, such as working memory, speed at a finger-tapping task, and demeanor. Based on previous human and animal studies, the researchers expected that the subjects' association of the environment with a positive experience—in this case, the extra dopamine releases caused by taking Ritalin—would result in faster movement, better memory and visual attention, and a more positive demeanor.

Extroverts who had taken Ritalin for the first three days of the study didn't show significant changes in subconscious traits when watching the films without the drug, and extroverts from the control group likewise did not react differently when the placebo was removed. This was precisely the result the researchers expected.

The phenomenon at play for the extroverts who had been part of the Ritalin group is called *associative conditioning*. By stimulating the participants' dopamine release/reward system for the first three days with Ritalin, when the fourth day came around, the extroverts in the group had been conditioned to associate contextual cues in the lab with the reward they were expecting, even when that reward was no longer present. This is just like Ivan Pavlov conditioning his poor dog to salivate, even when the food wasn't present.

As for the introverts? The control group showed no change when the placebo was removed, as was expected. When the researchers tested introverted subjects from the group that had been administered Ritalin, however, they found that the introverts showed little to no evidence of associative conditioning. After three days of experiencing elevated dopamine levels while watching the videos, removing the source of dopamine also removed all of its associated behavioral and demeanor changes.

What does this mean? Extroverts rely on their environment, while introverts do not. Extroverts are more sensitive to changes and use their immediate surroundings to orient themselves. Of course, we know that introverts are stuck in their prefrontal cortexes, for better or worse.

The research team at Cornell showed a crucial difference between the ways introverts and extroverts process stimulation, specifically feelings of excitement. The positive feelings and enjoyment of the videos experienced by the extroverts who received Ritalin were associated with their immediate environment, whereas introverts had milder reactions, or even no reactions at all, to the videos because they associate the same feelings of reward with inner thoughts or possibly even interpreted the feelings of reward as anxiety.

As one of the authors of the study, Richard A. Depue, put it, "At a broader level, the study begins to illuminate how individual differences in brain functioning interact with environmental influences to create behavioral variation."

For introverts, internal cues have a much stronger impact on state of mind than environmental influences and reward cues do. That's why the associative conditioning effects of Ritalin were only evident in extroverts, as it didn't translate into reward or motivation for the introverts.

Let's take Helen, an elderly Alzheimer's patient, as an example of how powerful associative conditioning can sometimes be. Helen was an extrovert through and through—a loud and proud Italian woman—whose decade-plus-long battle with dementia eventually led to her passing away. In the last couple years of her life, Helen forgot almost everything and everyone she had ever known, and it became increasingly difficult to help her feel happy and comfortable. When all else failed, though, there were still a couple things caregivers could do to help put her in a more positive mood.

One such tactic was to put on a DVD of her favorite television show, *Columbo*, an old detective show with episodes usually running well over an hour. Her short-term memory lasted a matter of mere minutes in those latter days, but she would still sit through the entire episode, chuckling at Detective Columbo's catchphrases and getting excited when he caught the murderer at the end—even though she couldn't follow along with the plot or even remember the name of the show. Through decades of watching and loving the show, the associated feelings of happiness and comfort had become deeply conditioned in her psyche to the point that even when her brain had deteriorated, the associative conditioning remained.

We can only wonder how Helen's final years may have been different if she was highly introverted instead. Based on the findings of the associative conditioning study, it's quite possible that her caregivers would have been even more helpless to do anything to improve her quality of life. Such is the power of how we process stimuli.

This study, along with the previous study on introverts having thicker prefrontal cortices, reinforces our earlier conclusion that extroverts live more in the moment than introverts do. While introverts are analyzing more and responding to internal stimuli, extroverts are relying more on instinct, which results in their surroundings having a greater influence on what they are currently seeing and feeling.

We can certainly learn a lot about a person by studying what motivates them—what rewards and stimulation they seek for themselves. For extroverts, these rewards may often be things such as making more positive connections, having adventures, and being positively stimulated by their environments. Introverts, on the other hand, might tend to be more motivated by feelings of fulfillment and satisfaction—

internally rewarding feelings. We can better understand how two people can be exposed to the same environment and turn out wildly different.

From a broader perspective, just the term *conditioning* is a reminder of how plastic our brains are and how external and internal stimuli are constantly changing and reshaping them. It's easy to go through life unaware of the long-term consequences of everything going on around you and in your own head—but those consequences do exist. We are products of our subconscious.

In 1999, scientists measured the cerebral blood flow of the two groups with positron emission tomography scans (PET) scans, while subjects thought about anything without instruction. They had similar findings; introverts and extroverts had the same amount of blood flow to their brains, but in different regions.

The frontal lobes and anterior thalamus of an introvert's brain, involved with recalling events, making plans, and solving problems, saw this flow more than any other part. It meant they preferred to interact and talk to themselves than to others because of how inward their brains had been wired. Again, this brain activity points to the typical behavior of an introvert.

Extroverts had more blood flow into the anterior cingulate gyrus, temporal lobes, and posterior thalamus—brain areas involved with interpreting sensory data. Extroverts also had less blood flow to brain areas associated with behavioral inhibition.

Therefore, they are focused on the activities of their surroundings and the people in them and don't think about limiting or censoring themselves. Their brains are designed to choose the greatest impact of activity for raising their arousal levels. Again, it explains why extroverts tend to be outgoing and can easily strike up conversations with anyone. They are focused outwards, while introverts are focused inwards.

All the research certainly shows a clear separation between introverts and extroverts. On one hand, you have someone who seeks out stimulation from the environment and people because it's as if they are wearing earplugs. On the other hand, you have someone who, in the same environment and social interaction, feels like they are wearing hearing aids.

Brain Chemicals

The next stop on our tour of the biological difference between introverts and extroverts is about the brain chemicals known as neurotransmitters. We briefly discussed dopamine earlier, but there are multiple ones at work here.

Unlike your favorite science fiction movie, these chemical differences don't create superheroes and villains. The neurotransmitters largely responsible for the difference between introverts and extroverts are *dopamine and acetylcholine.*

Let's tackle them one by one. Dopamine is a neurotransmitter that everyone produces in the brain in reaction to stimuli that we encounter in the world. Think about how we produce saliva according to whether we sense food around us.

Specifically, dopamine is released before (in anticipation), during, and after we receive *pleasurable* stimuli. It is the neurochemical associated with sex, drugs, and rock and roll. If there's a large slice of chocolate cake about to be devoured, dopamine is going to be released. Excited about finding a new beau? Cue the dopamine. Screaming on a rollercoaster? Equal parts dopamine and adrenaline, perhaps.

When a neuron releases dopamine to another neuron, the dopamine floats through the synapse; think of the brain's synapses as the highways between each neuron. These are the roads that the chemicals travel through to get to the receiving neuron. It may sound like an easy process, but our brains have countless neurons that are constantly firing. Different chemicals are being released every second to help an individual go about their day.

So what does this all mean? Dopamine signals pleasure, but different stimuli, situations, and individual perception can affect how dopamine is produced and distributed. Of course, depending on the personality of the individual, dopamine is also processed differently.

Research has shown that extroverts are less sensitive to dopamine than introverts (Scott Barry Kaufman, 2014). It was found that when exposed to the same reward stimulus, introverts were affected more, while extroverts needed a higher degree of intensity to elicit the same feelings.

Everyone craves dopamine, but extroverts need higher amounts to feel its effects, almost like someone who has developed a tolerance for caffeine or more illicit drugs. Therefore, to get enough dopamine to make an emotional impact, extroverts need greater or more rewards than introverts to create and process dopamine in their brains. It's as if the sensation has been dulled for extroverts, so they continually seek out stimuli to produce the results they crave.

This may partially explain why extroverts want to be around people and indeed are stereotypically found at the center of a party. The more stimuli and rewards that swirl around the extrovert, the higher the chance that they generate dopamine in sufficient quantities to effectively feel pleasure.

This brings additional clarity to what the extrovert is really after. Earlier, we discussed that they enjoy interaction though not necessarily connecting, and now we discover that extroverts are seeking adequate stimulation to *feel* something. That's reducing them to simple slaves to their brains' needs, which is not always true, but it's certainly food for thought as to what drives and fulfills them.

Introverts, on the other hand, are much more sensitive to dopamine. They do not require as much attention or stimulation to receive the amount of dopamine needed to feel pleasure. Because introverts are highly sensitive to dopamine, they may crave more alone and quiet time. Their main task is to avoid being overwhelmed by an excess of dopamine, and thus they sequester themselves to do so.

This sensitivity to dopamine means that for introverts, there *is* such a thing as "too much of a good thing." If extroverts need increasing amounts of dopamine to feel good, introverts need only subtle or small amounts. More than that, and you're looking at someone who wants to retreat, even if it's from their own birthday party.

This makes even more sense if we put things back into the context of the social battery we introduced earlier. Dopamine drains the social battery of the introvert, and thus introverts seek refuge while extroverts seek out dopamine-producing stimuli.

Additional supporting research has shown that the difference in dopamine sensitivity could be due to the number of dopamine receptors each individual has (Marti Laney).

In summary, extroverted individuals need much more dopamine to feel happy at the same level an introvert would feel from a smaller amount of dopamine. They need to seek attention, be social, and participate in stimulating activities to release the dopamine they need. Introverts are the opposite. If they get too much dopamine, they feel overwhelmed and anxious. They need more quiet time so that they are not overwhelming their dopamine receptors.

Dopamine is produced, processed, and dealt with differently in extroverts versus introverts.

Does this mean that introverts are destined for a brain that is set off by minimal amounts of dopamine or perpetually under-satisfied and on the verge of explosion? What, then, is pleasurable for the introvert?

Imagine you have just woken up on a sleepy Sunday morning. You go to the kitchen and make yourself a warm cup of tea. That first sip of tea warms you from the inside out. It makes you feel relaxed, calm, and content. That feeling is caused by the neurotransmitter *acetylcholine*, which is what introverts tend to prefer.

Acetylcholine is the opposite of adrenaline. When adrenaline is released, the body goes into fight-or-flight mode. Your senses become heightened, your heart rate goes through the roof, and you are ready for whatever comes your way. Acetylcholine takes you out of fight-or-flight mode. After you finish fighting off the threat or running for your life, it is the breath of fresh air that helps you relax and brings your bodily functions back to a normal state. It brings you to homeostasis.

In the central nervous system, acetylcholine is also used in conjunction with pleasure and rewards, though a different type of reward than dopamine signals. Acetylcholine makes us feel good when we turn inward and can focus on fewer things with fewer people. It makes us feel good when we are relaxed.

It should come as no surprise then that the activities introverts most enjoy release the soothing effect of acetylcholine. Engaging in activities that are low-key, calming, and mentally challenging releases acetylcholine.

Introverted brains have been shown to have increased blood flow through acetylcholine pathways, whereas extroverts have this blood flow on their dopamine pathways (Christine Fonseca). The dopamine pathway is also shorter than the acetylcholine pathway. It takes longer for someone to feel the pleasure associated with acetylcholine-inducing stimuli. This is all good and fine for the introvert who wants to be able to pace themselves, but for the extrovert? They get bigger rewards much faster when they receive a hit of dopamine versus acetylcholine.

Since they enjoy this quick and powerful happiness boost, why would they want to look elsewhere? They won't—they'll keep engaging in the types of behavior that can gain them dopamine, which are what we would recognize as typically extroverted behavior. As you can see, seeking pleasure and the subsequent manipulation of these neurotransmitters (albeit unknowingly) can lead to very characteristic behaviors.

Introverts crave acetylcholine because it's their most prevalent source of rewards, which are signaled by what we would recognize as typically introverted behavior—relaxed, calm, and slow-moving. Extroverts can still reflect and be lost in thought, but this pleasurable feeling from acetylcholine pales in comparison to the jolt of dopamine they require.

Extroverts handle an onslaught of stimulation masterfully. In fact, they thrive on and crave this stimulation that produces dopamine. Introverts are more sensitive to dopamine and crave the rewards acetylcholine provides, which correspond to opposing types of behaviors. Thus, extroverts need hearing aids on their dopamine receptors. Their receptors are not as sensitive, so they need to receive that much more to get a hit. The more dopamine they get, the better they feel.

On the opposite side of the spectrum, introverts need earplugs. Introverts are currently walking around with mega speakers on their dopamine receptors. Even a small amount can seem like too much. Their receptors are different than extroverts' in that they are more sensitive.

This all fits neatly with the social battery concept. Extroverts fill their batteries with the people they surround themselves with. Dopamine fills their battery up. Introverts recharge their batteries alone. When they receive dopamine, it can overflow and fry the social battery, and instead they seek the rewards that acetylcholine provides them with.

For introverts to be happy and thrive, they need to reduce the dopamine and increase the acetylcholine in their brains. This leads introverts to be selective about what they do and who they interact with, and eventually they retreat into solace. That's why pretending to be busy for an entire weekend, when in reality you are just at home by yourself with four books, can feel so good.

If you're an introvert, you know that you are walking around with an increased sensitivity to social situations courtesy of your dopamine tolerance. Just don't try to perform a pale imitation of an extrovert, because it's not in your biology to derive happiness from those behaviors. While blindfolds and earplugs may help, they're not always the most practical choice.

Be selective about your social interaction and try to find what's really exhausting you. Make sure to recharge alone so you can bask in the sweet glow of acetylcholine, which is what will actually make you happy.

Introverts and extroverts are who they are because of these chemical differences. It goes beyond preferences and personality; it is literally programmed into our brains.

The last major neurobiological difference is how *aroused* extroverts and introverts are in their natural states.

Background Noise

Hans Eysenck, the researcher that coined the term ambivert, also found that the brains of different personality types had different baseline levels of *cortical arousal*—the degree to which our minds are in motion and being stimulated, the level of static perpetually present. High cortical arousal is perhaps best illustrated by imagining your brain activity when you are unable to sleep. Sometimes this is positive, and other times it is negative.

Think of the brain like a power generator. Some are more active than others, which means they run at a higher level for no reason. Suppose a power generator runs at a level of 500 watts while on standby, while another power generator runs at a level of 50 watts while on standby. What accounts for this difference? It's unclear, and there is no clear reason other than the fact that these power generators are designed according to different blueprints. Both of these power generators stop functioning at a level of 1000 watts.

Eysenck found that the brain of an introvert has a higher level of baseline arousal; it's constantly busy and never turns off. For them, this is negative. The introvert is the power generator that runs at a background level of 500 watts, which means it is always active, alert, and analyzing.

However, it's also much closer to the limit of 1000 watts, which means it can more easily be overwhelmed, blow up, and shut down. In fact, it has to be careful of how much stimulation it gets, otherwise it just might shut down from external interference and overloading the circuits. For the introvert, this can be too much social interaction, conversation, or the presence of people in general.

Extroverts, on the other hand, can handle being surrounded by people and loud noises. They're only starting at 50 watts, after all. They don't need time to unplug and recharge alone after social interactions. Instead, they are only minimally stimulated, so they are actively seeking out highly stimulating environments to raise their arousal levels. Moreover, it takes a larger number of stimuli because of their blunted reaction to dopamine.

Make no mistake: it's not necessarily a positive aspect for the brain of an introvert to have a greater baseline level of arousal. It doesn't mean they are constantly at a higher level of cognitive performance. Would you say that someone who is more easily stressed out is lucky and should be characterized as smarter? No—you would see it for what it is: a trait that has both negative and positive connotations. This also doesn't mean extroverts aren't aware of their surroundings and capable of constant thought.

What does this difference in baseline arousal mean for us?

Sometimes, we just can't help how we are wired. Introverts have to pace themselves a bit more and make sure to keep their average usage rate lower because they are starting from a different point than extroverts are. As always, alone time is one of the best tools for regulating their levels of arousal and ensuring they don't become overwhelming. Extroverts have more leeway in social situations, which leads them to enjoy those situations more.

The reticular activating system (RAS) acts in a way that confirms Eysenck's findings in a major way. The RAS is responsible for regulating your levels of alertness and arousal. Assuming all humans need some type of arousal in their day, it explains why extroverts tend to act out or look for conversation with other people. On the other hand, introverts have a high level of activity in the RAS. They don't require any other stimulation to keep them going.

Studies have also found that the RAS can measure your baseline levels of arousal and even predict how much of an introvert or extrovert you would perceive yourself to be. If you have an active RAS, you are likely to respond in a greater way to external stimuli. That sounds curiously like the description of the introvert we have talked about multiple times in this book.

Eysenck devised what was imaginatively called the *lemon juice test*. The theory was that if someone's RAS was more sensitive and had a higher amount of activity, lemon juice squirted onto someone's tongue would produce more saliva than someone who had a less sensitive RAS.

In other words, the more saliva someone produces, the more likely they are an introvert because of an increased level of arousal and reaction to external stimuli. As Eysenck predicted, the introverts in the studies produced 50% more saliva than the extroverts. Introverts might just have a higher sensitivity to *everything* that comes their way.

The fact that something as small as drops of lemon juice can trigger massively different levels of reaction demonstrates the significance of baseline levels of arousal. A drop of lemon juice is nothing compared to a wild, raging party and meeting 20 new people. This puts the introvert in a totally different and more sympathetic light. What the extrovert might barely feel, the introvert might feel at a magnification of ×100.

Just think of the introvert and extrovert at a party. A simple conversation is going to have a bigger impact on the introvert because of their increased level of baseline arousal. It functions on the same principle as the lemon juice. Extroverts require a much larger stimulus to react and therefore would require far more lemon juice to produce the same amount of saliva.

Another helpful analogy is to compare extroverts to a steel wall and introverts to a glass window. Obviously, it is going to take less impact to break the glass window, and thus, introverts are more sensitive because of their inherent build.

How Did Introverts Survive Evolution?

In our fast-paced, competitive society, it's easy to imagine that the social fragility of introverts is a fatal character flaw. These biological differences can lead to a vision of an early hominid that was fearful, easily spooked, and generally a pushover. This translates into the modern day as well.

Here's the thinking: extroverts get all the toys because they're able to interact with other people more successfully and are more aggressive about getting what they want. Introverts, on the other hand, are perceived as being shy and less likely to enjoy the advantages of the world because they *don't* always mix with others. Growing tired of social interaction is so undesirable as a trait that pharmaceutical companies produce drugs for people to conquer it.

This thinking might cause those of us who muse about Darwinism and survival of the fittest to wonder, "If introverts are resistant or unable to be assertive about getting the spoils, how did they make it this far on earth? They should have been swallowed up by T. Rex long ago!"

But science suggests that not only did introverts' tendencies not get them killed, but they may have helped them *survive*.

Biologists who specialize in evolutionary theory divide the animal kingdom into two categories: "rovers" and "sitters." These labels correspond to an animal's tendencies in regard to moving about in the world.

Rovers are the bold ones. They're eager to examine the immediate landscape and explore the outer edges of their environment. Rovers are the ones who go out and kill for food and bring it back to their households. They're the type-As in their circles or groups. They go seize what they want.

Sitters, on the other hand, are in no hurry to venture out of their caves. They patiently wait until there's really nothing going on outside before they leave. They're content to sit at home and let the rovers bring home take-out food. Sitters couldn't care less if they don't jump all over the savannah, participate in hunting, or get a spot on

Animal Planet. Let the rovers get the spotlight.

So in our rush to toss out labels in the animal kingdom, we'd call the rovers more likely to be bold about entering society and therefore more likely to survive and adapt than the reclusive, overcautious sitters.

But here's the thing: rovers are also the first in line to get savagely eaten. Sure, they may be bold and unafraid to walk freely in the wild. But that leaves them open to predators who have been hiding in the background, patiently waiting for some poor roving sucker to cross their line of vision. When that happens, the rover is history.

Meanwhile, as the rover is being turned into a main-course meal with a side vegetable, the sitter is relaxation in their home, safe, sound, and not somebody else's dinner.

Hopefully it's not too hard to see how this relationship translates into human extroverts and introverts. Extroverts have more fun (or at least look like they are), are friendlier, and take more risks, whereas introverts act out of an abundance of caution. They don't jump into new situations head-first. They may appear to be sticks in the mud because they're not aggressive about socializing. This keeps them safe and secure and out of harm's way.

There's a dark side to extroverts, however. Daniel Nettle, a British evolutional psychologist, found that their adventurism comes at a price. He found that extroverts are more likely to get physically injured as a result of their escapades. They're also more likely to have extramarital affairs or switch out relationship partners. A study of bus drivers in 1963 found that bus drivers with "high extroversion scores" were far more likely to be in traffic accidents.

Introverts may show a certain social reticence, but they're still alive. In fact, their habit of appraising a situation before they enter into it makes them more skillful at team-leading, according to the Wharton Business School. Introverts are disproportionately *more* likely to get college degrees, Phi Beta Kappa keys, and National Merit Scholarships.

It turns out that introverts' social disinterest may serve a purpose. For example, when a child is chastised for misbehavior, it unlocks an anxiety and a mild fear of being punished for future transgressions. This helps them evolve into more careful beings, slightly more analytical about their place in the environment. Therefore, it makes them more likely to survive because of their own discretion.

An effective society is made up of a reasonable balance of introverts and extroverts—rovers and sitters as well. Neither group would survive on their own. But the idea that extroverts are better equipped to preserve order than shy, secluded introverts is a common misconception. They have far more influence in the continued sustenance and preservation of society. The fact that our species is still around today is in no small part due to over-analysis, rumination, caution, and occasional paralysis to stay out of the grasp of danger.

Takeaways:

- This chapter is a look at the different biological differences that place people where they are on the introvert/extrovert spectrum. No matter what someone's behavior is, it will always start from a baseline that their biology has set.
- The first biological difference is that introverts have denser brain matter in the prefrontal cortex, which is where analysis, ruminating, decision-making, and planning take place. In fact, it's where most stereotypical introverted behaviors take place. It also explains why introverts are said to be focused more on their internal worlds versus the external world—because they are literally stuck in their thoughts more than extroverts. To support this, extroverts were shown to have increased blood flow to areas involved

in sensory processing, which allows them to focus on their external world.

- Dopamine and acetylcholine are at the heart of another difference in how introverts and extroverts process external stimuli. Extroverts have blunted dopamine receptors, so they need more stimulation to feel pleasure. Introverts have heightened dopamine receptors, so they feel overwhelmed more easily. This leads them to seek out activities and behaviors that generate acetylcholine, which creates feelings of tranquility and calm.

- The final major biological difference is the level of background noise that is inside the introvert's or extrovert's mind. To put it plainly, introverts have perpetual static and chatter in their mind, which makes them more liable to overwhelm, analysis, rumination, and retreating to solitude. Hans Eysenck proved a corollary of this with his lemon juice test, in which he found that introverts were generally easier to arouse and become alert.

- All of these differences make it seem like introverts are somewhat less predisposed to survival than extroverts. But the opposite is true; zoological studies have found that there are generally two groups in a society, rovers and sitters, and both are needed because they complement each other. Rovers are extroverts—thrill-seekers and out and about. Sitters are introverts—planners, analyzers, and operating in the background. That is to say, introverts keep themselves and the people around them safer than they might be otherwise.

Chapter 3. The Pursuit of Happiness

Generally speaking, happiness is a feeling or a state of being that encompasses contentment, pleasure, joy, satisfaction, fulfillment, and well-being. We can definite it any number of ways, but we all want it and will go to the ends of the earth searching for happiness. Or at least to avoid *unhappiness*. The jury is still out on which of the two is more motivating.

Most of the time, a person's happiness is thought of as a primary component of their general temperament. "They're just a happy person" or "They're kind of a buzzkill" aren't rare things to hear. A person's happiness can also be a product of people's experiences, current mood, or simply the faces that they allow others to see. It's a multifaceted trait that, like most things, cannot be defined in by a single quantity alone.

Surprisingly, where you find yourself on the introvert/extrovert spectrum also seems to have a marked effect on your overall happiness.

Are there measurable differences in happiness between introverts and extroverts? Who is destined for a happier, more fulfilling life? Can how our social batteries recharge truly be responsible for happiness? Well, to start with, it doesn't only apply to human beings, which lends credence to this correlation.

As it turns out, certain animal groups also exhibit differences in social assertiveness and aggression. Take, for example, ring-tailed lemurs. Irish researcher Ipek Kulahci examined them for several years at a lemur program in the state of Georgia. She observed their behaviors in a few areas:

aggression, grooming, contact calling, and the ever-popular scent-marking.

It turns out lemurs have personalities and are also divisible by whether they're extroverts and introverts. The more social, extroverted lemurs were much more involved in excitable interactions—but they also had a tendency to get into more fights than others. You might characterize them as having higher highs and lower lows than more introverted lemurs.

Studies on gorillas have also found marked differences between gorillas of different personalities—this time in relation to overall lifespan. This was confirmed in a 2012 study by the University of Edinburgh, who studied the temperaments of 298 gorillas in captivity over the course of 18 years.

Researchers found that gorillas who were extroverted—those who showed curiosity, gregariousness, and playfulness—were the ones who lived longer lives, regardless of gender or any other factor. The findings fell in line with an early 2012 study of humans who had lived past the age of 100. That study, too, declared that extroverts and positive people were more likely to hit triple digits in age than those with introversion and more social isolation.

At this point, your intuition is probably telling you that extroverts are happier in general—and your intuition is correct.

Extroverts have an innate desire for a higher quantity and greater intensity of interpersonal interaction. They are generally more active, seek out stimulation more often, and have a high capacity for joy. People who identify as extroverts are often described as sociable, active, talkative, person-oriented, optimistic, fun-loving, and affectionate. Typical descriptions of introverts, on the other hand, include "reserved, sober, exuberant, aloof, task-oriented, retiring, and quiet."

Of the two, extroverts quite clearly sound like they would be more drawn to happiness and joy or at least experiences that create those emotions. They're out and about and have more opportunities to experience joy and amazing circumstances involving others. You'll read later on that extroverts self-report as having more relationships and sexual encounters, which supports that assertion. If happiness is at all related to the external world, then the extrovert has quite a leg up in terms of exposure and opportunity. There's the old saying that *showing up is half the battle*, and extroverts certainly fulfill that requirement.

But perhaps extroverts are merely more comfortable expressing themselves openly, while introverts don't share as readily. If one group is predisposed to be more social and open, it would make sense that they appear more emotional. Thus, are extroverts merely paying lip service and being more emotionally expressive, though not necessarily better off?

Time and again, behavioral psychologists have found that extroverts who take well-being surveys self-report as being happier than introverts do on the same surveys. Such studies can be informative; however, we can't necessarily accept them at face value, given that the results are self-reported and extroverts are inherently more likely than introverts to describe themselves as happy.

Typically, surveys having to do with personality type focus on five core personality traits that were researched and developed by D.W. Fiske beginning in 1949 and have become more widely supported since that time. These have since become known as the big five personality traits, and the model of viewing personality in five separate scales has gained widespread acceptance. Each trait functions on its own scale. As it happens, the big five personality traits and the Myers-Briggs type indicator are the two most prominent ways in which introversion or extroversion is defined and measured.

You can use the acronym OCEAN to help you remember the five traits, as listed and described below.

Openness to experience (inventive/curious vs. consistent/cautious). Would you be willing to take a chance on a big career opportunity if it requires moving to a new city and starting over with a new social circle? What about showing up to a party where you only know the host or perhaps nobody at all?

Conscientiousness (efficient/organized vs. easy-going/careless). How much time do you spend planning and organizing your life? Do you consistently reflect on goals and desires for personal outcomes, or do you prefer to just be yourself and do what comes naturally and let the rest work itself out?

Extroversion (outgoing/energetic vs. solitary/reserved). Does socializing typically energize or drain you? Do you prefer external stimulation, or do you spend a lot of time analyzing and introspecting? Of course, this is the personality trait we are most interested in measuring; it simply can't be done in a vacuum without giving consideration to other traits.

Agreeableness (friendly/compassionate vs. challenging/detached). Do you tend to get along with most people you socialize with and always prefer positive interactions? Do you often challenge people when you engage with them? Do you prefer to remain detached and unemotional in social interaction?

*Neuroticism (sensitive/nervous vs. secure/confident). A*re you sensitive to how people perceive and think about you? Does interacting with people you aren't comfortable with make you nervous? Or are you generally secure in yourself and confident in social situations?

Ryan Howell, a psychologist from San Francisco State University, conducted a study that may lend more insight on this subject. Seven hundred fifty-four students were identified as being more introverted or extroverted, then asked to a complete a series of online questionnaires on personality, life satisfaction, and personal memories.

The results of the study showed that those individuals who identified as extroverts were more likely to recall good things from the past and downplay the bad relative to the introverts studied. Moreover, this positive outlook on past experiences explained the 45% correlation between extroversion and greater life satisfaction. For more neurotic types, the tendency to take a more negative view of the past explained the 50% correlation between their personality type and happiness level.

What can we conclude from this? The findings of this study essentially show that extroverts have a special tip for being happier and more optimistic—they literally *forget* negativity or otherwise choose not to fixate on it. They experience it, to be sure, but it either doesn't stick in their long-term memory or it doesn't ruin their outlook and memories.

Does this mean they had happier lives? Not necessarily. Perhaps they *did* as a result of extroverted tendencies that placed them into happiness's path, or perhaps there's something about increased socialization that allows extroverts to mentally move onto greener pastures, so to speak.

This whole concept will be foreign to introverts. It certainly sounds nice in theory to focus on the positives and forget the negatives in life, but that's not a conscious choice they can make. Recall that introverts have the tendency to be stuck in their own heads, without the natural impulse to seek support and positivity from their environments. If introverts are somewhat more resistant to the influences of the external world, then they have nothing to soothe them and either remind them that everything is going to be alright or point out the bright side of things.

So extroverts self-report as happier and more fulfilled. Is there anything we can do to even the scales? Can introverts only understand that their very nature compounds negativity and decreases happiness? If the goal is happiness, introverts should attempt to let things go. This can often end up feeling like you are just suggesting that someone grow taller or change their facial structure—it seems rather dreary and bleak, but it reflects reality.

We've now established some evidence that extroverts are indeed happier, whether it's because of their life perspective or their greater number of opportunities for happy occasions. Psychologists Wido Oerlemans and Arnold Bakker also conducted a study exploring the link between happiness and extroversion—this time focusing on how different actions impact introverts and extroverts.

They recruited more than 1,300 people and asked them to keep track of their daily activities and to describe their feelings at the time. When the final tallies came in, they had collected data on nearly 14,000 activities across some 5,600 days.

The researchers found that different types of activities were more meaningful depending on whether you are an introvert or extrovert. Extroverts particularly favored "rewarding" activities like being paid to work, exercising, or winning a competition. When these rewarding activities were coupled with social interaction, the subsequent happiness level rose even higher.

On the opposite side of the spectrum, introverts were more responsive to punishments and other negative situations, which made them unhappier. Extroverts were more emotionally affected by positivity and happiness, while introverts were more emotionally affected by negativity and unhappiness.

The theory that extroverts are happier as a result of being more responsive to rewards was first published by Gray in 1982. The theory was later supported by Larsen and Ketelaar in 1991 when their research found that extroverts consistently reacted more strongly to positive situations than introverts did.

It's a theme we're beginning to see develop: introverts are not wired to look on the bright side of things. If you were constantly scanning and analyzing, you might not either. It's as if an extrovert's mood could be raised by receiving ice cream, whereas it would take a five-course meal to raise the introvert's mood—positivity doesn't move the needle for the introvert nearly as much.

But overall, this might not be a statement about happiness, but rather probability. A study conducted in 1985 by Headey found that extroverted people have greater chances to experience favorable events—like falling in love, for example—in their lives. Extroverts engage in more interaction and experiences in general, so it follows that they will have more positive experiences as well.

This is actually encouraging. Less socially active individuals who want to be happier can bring more happiness into their lives by simply being more willing to go out and engage. Increasing the sheer volume of experiences doesn't ensure that all of them will be positive, but a proportionate amount probably will be, which increases the amount of happiness you will experience overall, regardless of your personality type.

If confidence and social skills do not come naturally to you, or if you simply want more of them, these are things that can be practiced and improved upon, regardless of your personality type.

Take, for example, the story of one Jason Comely, originator of *rejection therapy*. After his wife left him for another man, Jason found himself unhappy and withdrawn from life, rarely socializing at all. He realized that his isolated lifestyle was exceedingly unhealthy and stemmed from a fear of rejection.

So what did Jason do? Every single day for one year, Jason purposefully got rejected. In doing so, he overcame his fear of rejection and became increasingly more confident and outgoing, reclaiming his happiness along the way. Jason's story may be a little extreme, but it provides one source of social proof that simply making the effort to engage in more social activity can have positive effects on your well-being and happiness.

A more recent study, conducted in 2012 by Zelenski, Santoro, and Whelan, resulted in perhaps the most interesting findings.

Like in the previously mentioned studies, these researchers found that the extroverted way of thinking did indeed create more happiness. Contrary to the other studies, however, Zeleneski did not ask participants to answer questions based on their personality types and position on the extrovert/introvert spectrum. Instead, they had all of the participants use a script to behave as stereotypical extroverts and another script to behave as stereotypical introverts. They found that both the extroverts and introverts in the study reported feeling happier when they acted like extroverts. This would appear to definitively proclaim extroverts as the happier personality type.

Unfortunately, when we take a deeper look at the design of the study, we see that this may not be the case still.

When the participants were behaving as extroverts, they were told to be *bold, talkative, energetic, active,* and *assertive.* Fair enough. But when it came time to take on the behavior of introverts, participants received a script that instructed them to be *reserved, quiet, lethargic, passive, compliant,* and *unadventurous.*

This represents an antiquated version of introversion and does not accurately describe many people who have mostly introverted tendencies. It's a negative stereotype that we have proven is simply untrue. There are few, if any, people in this world who actively desire to be lethargic, passive, compliant, and unadventurous, don't you think?

Contrary to the script, introverts can certainly be talkative—and as you may have observed, there are many who are. And if you get an introvert talking about something that they are passionate about, they can be as energetic and assertive as anybody else. To be a truly definitive study, it would have evaluated people based only on their social capacity—what they do when they are tired, when their social battery is low.

That being said, we shouldn't dismiss the study altogether. Putting the information from all of the studies mentioned in this chapter together, what can we say about the pursuit of happiness?

If you're an extrovert, just being yourself and consistently seeking out social engagement ought to do the trick. For introverts, on the other hand, if you don't want to increase your volume of social interaction, you can change how effectively that interaction results in your happiness by behaving more similarly to an extrovert. Rather than analyzing and thinking your way through, try to be present in the moment and engage energetically and confidently with the people around you. People will receive you better, and you will literally feel better by trying to embody those traits.

Another factor to consider in this grand equation of happiness is the role that being accepted in society plays. Western societies certainly seem to value extroversion and its associated behaviors above introversion, and so extroverts may naturally feel better knowing that they fit the ideal mold. They don't feel the need to change themselves. This works the opposite way for introverts—they can be made to feel as if they need to change or, worse, fake their personalities to be accepted.

It does seem that extroverts have the edge when it comes to happiness. Indeed, the last study proved that popular conception of extroverts is positive, while our conception of introverts is moody at best.

Lest you think that happiness is what matters, there is one final wrinkle: too much sociability doesn't mean that every day is a never-ending party.

Consider the primary objective of the introvert when they are tired: staying at home and watching television alone. While that kind of quiet relaxation certainly has its benefits, scientists have found that too much social isolation can be a significant health risk. And this is something that comes all too naturally to introverts.

Brigham Young University researcher Julianne Holt-Lunstad reviewed data from a large number of health studies that included results from over three million people. These studies specifically contained information pertaining to loneliness, social isolation, and living by one's self. Unsurprisingly, she found that people in active relationships experienced healthier lives and courted fewer risks to their well-being than those who were isolated.

In fact, Holt-Lunstad's findings contained at least a degree of alarm. She found that the mortality risk of lonely people is as serious as those of alcoholics or moderate smokers. Even worse, lonely people are *more* likely to face an early demise than people suffering from obesity. She also determined that young people who are closed are *more* susceptible to health dangers than older people who lived alone.

Having simulated closeness with others online didn't help much, either. Holt-Lunstad found that romantic relationships were actually damaged if the couple engaged in text messaging more than actual, up-close and personal communication. Sorry, introverts. Picking up the phone and making plans is sometimes necessary.

However, the other extreme—having a limitless supply of social contacts—isn't healthy either, according to renown anthropologist Robin Dunbar. He analyzed data from a staggering six billion telephone conversations from an unidentified country in Europe. After filtering out business calls—as well as calls from people who just didn't use the phone that often—Dunbar looked for patterns in how many times people returned phone calls from certain people.

Dunbar had earlier claimed that the average person could only manage consistent social relationships with 150 people at one time (with some people being closer than others, of course). The results from Dunbar's telephone survey, however, claimed that when it comes to closer, personal friendships, we can only really handle about *five* of them at any given time. That's about as many people as you could fit into a compact car with a reasonable degree of comfort, driver included. It almost makes it seem like extroverts are using a lot of wasted motion and energy when they can only really have five close friends anyway. Of course, that doesn't mean they are any less happy.

A Change of Mind

It seems that no matter how you slice it, extroverts are living happier and more fulfilling lives. This leads to a natural question: can you truly change yourself—extrovert to introvert or introvert to extrovert?

Is it possible? Well, sort of. It even occurs naturally as we age. We change as a result of emotional maturation. There are studies to back up the stereotypes of the gentle grandma and the mellowed-out grandfather. With enough time, change is inevitable.

But what about *right now*? People have been altering themselves to some degree for all of history in the interest of psychological and physical survival. The ability to change personality styles to operate on the other side of the extroversion/introversion spectrum would give you the flexibility to operate in the ever-changing environment of work and even in your family life.

But that sounds more like changing your behaviors and putting on a mask for different contexts, not your underlying personality and temperament. Is the latter possible? As you've read, we are born with literally different brain structures that would seemingly make it difficult to change.

The notion of changing our brain structures is best encapsulated in the principle of *brain plasticity*, which is the notion that change is possible all throughout life.

During the 1990s, Alvaro Paschal-Leone of Harvard Medical School conducted experiments in which brain scans were used to measure changes in the neural networks in the brain. He noted changes that took place in seniors who had suffered strokes. New networks of neural connections actually grew in order to adapt to changes in the person's mental environment.

The new networks typically formed in adjacent areas of the brain due to the activity of the glial cells that support neurons. This process of growing new neural networks to replace damaged ones is called "cortical remapping." Whatever brain structures were crippled during the stroke were compensated for. If the brain can change to rejuvenate stroke victims, then surely we can change aspects of our personalities, right?

Researchers have noted that soldiers who lost limbs in war manifested the growth of new neural networks in their brains in order to adapt to prostheses. Other people also exhibit strange and subtle changes, such as the hippocampus of London taxi drivers being denser and larger than the average person—because the hippocampus is where long-term memory is formed and stored, and taxi drivers have to remember maps and locations.

It's possible to change the brain's structure and behavior. The primary purpose of psychotherapy is to help people make positive changes in their lives. Psychologists know that people can consciously change themselves for the better. The entire field of cognitive psychology has been borne as a result of that discovery about neuroplasticity.

The question still remains—even if the brain structure can change for beneficial purposes, can it change to serve an arbitrary purpose such as becoming more extroverted or introverted? Can we create change in the dopamine and acetylcholine receptors, as well as turn down the background static present in the introverted mind?

Take Maureen. As a person and as an actress, Maureen had achieved the reputation of being a demure, quiet, and laid-back person. In fact, she rated quite high on the introverted personality trait scale. She was always cast in subservient roles. All her fellow actresses and actors in the company were shocked when the casting director chose Maureen for the main character in *Jane Eyre*. However, in the role, Maureen excelled and stole the hearts of the audience. People were crying and clapping after the performance. There were standing ovations, and the show was even extended from a week to a week and a half.

If Maureen were to perform this role and the associated duties, would she change her personality or would she be perpetually tired and socially exhausted?

Despite the fact that this sounds like brain plasticity, is it? Is this truly a representation of changing someone's personality and temperament, or is it just adapting to a new circumstance when needed and regressing to the mean when it is *not* needed?

In a 2015 study addressing personality change, Nathan Hudson and Christopher Fraley of the University of Illinois at Urbana-Champaign gave undergraduates a 16-week intensive course intended to act as an intervention toward effecting a personality change. The students were asked if they wanted to change some of their personality traits. They responded in the affirmative.

Results of a program for behavior change that centered on coaching and intervention showed that the subjects who wanted to change actually *did* change in all but one of the personality factors (openness to new experiences). The statistical change found in extroversion was especially powerful.

When we take a step back and consider how monumental this finding was, consider how we battle things like anxiety or phobias. They can also be said to be personality traits because they govern the way we think, they can often define us, and they have some sort of biological basis. With stress and anxiety, cortisol and adrenaline flood the nervous system far too often; for phobias, adrenaline is triggered at the slightest hint of danger.

And yet people conquer those things every day. So perhaps it's not so surprising that we can truly change aspects of our personality if we approach them like defeating a phobia—or something more detrimental to our lives that would make us truly motivated to solve it.

The key to change, as noted by Hudson and Fraley, was to make a specific behavior change *plan*. Don't just say you're going to be "more outgoing and sociable" or that you will try to see the good in people even when you're socially fatigued.

Instead decide that on a particular day you will make the effort to initiate an interaction with someone else whom you don't know very well. Perhaps you could contact that person and meet up somewhere. The more details, the better, and the harder it is to stop trying. Quantify your efforts, make them measurable, and fulfill them on schedule—this is what an effective plan consists of.

This is exactly what it takes to tackle phobias and anxiety. It's a process known as exposure therapy or incremental exposure, and it is a gradual plan that requires consistency to achieve behavior change. It can take months or even years to change the brain structure (specifically neurotransmitter production here) and eventually change the subsequent behavior. This is something we can take cues from for our quest in changing our temperament trait.

It's not something we think to apply this type of rigid structure to, but it's only because it doesn't occur. Personality change is possible if you treat it like a project or habit and work hard at it. We can't do it off the cuff just by wishing for it; we have to put the work in for actual brain plasticity to occur. Bad habits also stem from the same type of consistency and drive—only they are detrimental to us and we do them subconsciously because they are easy.

Change intervention, such as created in Hudson and Fraley's study, was additionally unsuccessful if one's motivation to change was too general. Thus, in addition to being persistent and consistent, you must keep in mind what your end goal is and understand that the setbacks or pains you are currently facing are temporary and passing. Without a light at the end of the tunnel, any type of change can feel hopeless and ultimately impossible.

There appear to be two options: we can create habits that will propel us into behavior and personality change, or we can just wait it out. Recall the stereotypes of the elderly—comfortable, open, kind, and generous. Are there actual patterns of personality and happiness change throughout the processing of aging?

A 2017 study by Northwestern University's Eileen Grant reviewed data from 14 previous personality studies that covered over 47,000 individuals. Some of the subjects had been monitored over long periods of time, as much as several decades. The traits are encapsulated in OCEAN (as a reminder: openness to conscientiousness, extroversion, agreeableness, and neuroticism).

Grant sought out how much people changed in one of the big five personality traits over the course of their lifetimes. She determined that in elderly people, no less than *four* of these five personality traits tend to *decline* over the course of a lifetime, by about 1–2% every decade. The sole holdout was "agreeableness," which appeared to remain steady overall, but that was because Grant found the data went in either direction—people either became more agreeable or less agreeable, so the results evened out.

But the other four characteristics tend to decline over the span of a lifetime. People become more emotionally strong, less sociable, less open-minded, and less organized as they get older. More specifically, we become less open, less conscientious, less extroverted, and less neurotic (except really late in life when we're about to die—*then* we tend to get a bit nervous, understandably so). And we also get less extroverted and more withdrawn.

We can make a few guesses about why this might be. We typically have fewer and fewer responsibilities at an advanced age. We work less, subject ourselves to discomfort less, and generally become more isolated. We are set in our ways not because we are incapable of learning, but because we are simply less willing to do so. We stop caring about pleasing others and become more self-focused on what we know makes us happy.

The elderly people she showed decreased in most of the trait scales over the run of their lifetime, but when Grant limited her findings to what happened when people went from youth to middle age, there were different changes. They also showed significant personality change, but they tended to demonstrate an *increase* in three of the key traits: conscientiousness, openness, and extroversion.

What causes *this* change? Once again, we are left to making guesses based on typical young adult life events and stages. Everything that is involved in establishing oneself—seeking a career, meeting new people, finding a romantic partner, and aspiring to become someone you want to be—involves these three traits. At this point in your life, people are typically still trying to conform to the world around them instead of being happy and working the opposite way.

That's right, introverts. You just might open up and become more socially resistant in your young adult and middle years, but statistics show that growing older will close the loop and bring you back to where you started. Personality change is possible, even natural and inevitable. But in order to direct it toward what you want and not just the creation of bad habits, you must be diligent in creating a plan of action.

If you feel that introversion is truly holding you back from happiness, there's hope. Professor Brian Little of Cambridge University further emphasized the possibility of change in what he coined *free trait theory*.

He proposed that one's personality is somewhat determined by their upbringing. Those constructs he called the *biogenic factors*. He believes that your childhood and early life experiences shape your personality to some extent. However, Little introduced new traits that he indicated modified the influence of biogenic factors. Little called these *idiogenic factors*. They have to do with personal choice and the motivation to change. When we are properly motivated with enough pain or pleasure, we can change. That is the crux of free trait theory—traits are free to come or go based on proper motivation. This notion might be even more empowering than seeing someone who was terrified of spiders conquer their phobia and gently pick one up with no hesitation. On some level, who we are is all a choice. It's whether we care enough to make the choices that we want, instead of the choice that is easy.

Takeaways:

- Happiness—it is different for everyone, and the only thing we know is that we want it. That, or we want to avoid unhappiness; either will suffice most of the time. There is a marked difference in happiness levels between introverts (sadder) and extroverts (happier). You might consider two paths: (1) extroverts have a greater probability of being exposed to happiness-inducing events or (2) extrovert tendencies stemming from biological differences cause extroverts to evaluate their lives in more positive ways.
- With the difference in happiness, a natural question becomes whether introverts can change their personalities to be more extroverted and thus happier. The answer? Yes. If people can

overcome phobias and traumatic brain injuries such as a stroke, they can also create neural change in personalities. But it takes commitment, a plan, and strong motivation like any change.

- Aging also changes the personality—four out of the five big five personality traits were found to decrease with age, though not before increasing for a spell during young adulthood.

Chapter 4. The Science of Introversion

If there's only one theme for you to take away from this book thus far, it should be that introversion and extroversion decide more than who likes to chatter.

You've read about differences in brain chemistry and structure and even what type of personality lends itself better to love and romance. There are many other small differences that define people on the personality spectrum, and many are counterintuitive aspects you would never think of.

We've gone over many stereotypes of the personality types, and some of these differences emphasize these typical behaviors and some do the opposite and dispel them. Whatever the case, the goal of this chapter is to gain additional insight into your particular personality. If you're anything like me, you'll proclaim, "That is totally me," at least twice while reading. The personality spectrum, at least in terms of social interest, is representative of how complex and subconscious our actions can be.

This chapter presents much of the current science about introverts and what that says about them (us).

Quiet Judgment

On first instinct, who do you suppose might be more judgmental: introverts or extroverts?

All the signs are there for introverts to be more judgmental, if you are being honest with yourself. They are routinely characterized as inward-focused, analytical, and more reserved. Additionally, they grow sick and tired of people easily because their social batteries run low but also likely because they think people aren't worth growing fatigued for. A 2016 study by Boland and Queen put this theory to the test and confirmed that introverts tend to pass judgment more easily on others.

They did this by testing how participants reacted to grammatical errors and typos in emails. Some of the emails had zero errors, while others were riddled with mistakes. The participants were asked to rate the authors of the emails with questions such as "the writer seems friendly" or "the writer seems considerate and trustworthy."

Meanwhile, the participants also filled out a personality questionnaire that was a version of the big five personality traits, which were described earlier: openness, conscientiousness, extroversion, agreeableness, and neuroticism. Of course, for our purposes, the researchers focused on extroversion or lack thereof.

They found that introverts were far more likely than extroverts to rate people poorly in the questions, saying they were less friendly, less considerate, and less trustworthy overall. The extroverts rated the error-free and error-riddled emails roughly the same, while there was a marked dip from the introverts where applicable.

Besides introverts universally caring more about grammar (questionable), the only conclusion we can draw is that introverts are indeed more judgmental. In the event they don't just care more about spelling and grammar, introverts are quick to impose judgment on someone based on little to no information about them.

A typo can occur for many reasons, and the introverts didn't give the benefit of the doubt—they simply leapt to the conclusion that the author of such typos would be less trustworthy and less friendly. It seems harsh, and while they're not necessarily wrong, it's a specific way of evaluating others arbitrarily.

Ignoring the results of this study, are introverts actually more judgmental? If you think about it, they possess all the traits of someone that does judge. They analyze, they think to themselves, they watch, and they tend to think heavily before acting. They spend a lot of time with themselves— what they speak might only be a fraction of what is thought, so it stands to reason that they feel they use their words wisely.

In other words, they believe they make relatively intelligent and measured decisions and judge those who don't appear to do the same. Perhaps they expect that everyone places the same value on how they appear to others; in the same vein, we can probably expect that introverts are more vain and self-conscious about what others think of them. Maybe that's where the stereotype of the meek and adventure-averse introvert comes from, despite how wrong it is.

To introverts, it's not just an errant error; it's a mental shortcoming to not think before acting. Even though we've talked about extroverts being more affected by their external environments, it appears that the introverts judge it more harshly.

Caffeine Addiction

How many of us would call ourselves caffeine addicts without batting an eye? If we're not in it for the supposed boost in alertness and performance, perhaps we're just in it for the ritual and smell of roasted coffee beans. Whatever the case, coffee is a nearly inescapable part of many of our lives.

If you classify yourself as both an introvert and a caffeine addict, you might want to rethink your strategies on waking up in the morning. A recent theory by Brian Little, the same Brian Little who originated the *free trait theory*, proposed that caffeine can actually be detrimental to the performance of an introvert and cause them to overload as if their social battery was fully drained and fatigued.

Considering the information we've learned throughout the book, this doesn't necessarily come as a surprise.

First, recall that introverts have a higher baseline level of arousal. That means they are more easily overstimulated and have a lower tolerance for social interaction. The power plant is already humming at high capacity and prone to overheating. Second, recall the studies that have shown that alcohol is particularly effective in changing introverts' temperaments. Third, we've made the comparison that introverts are walking around with giant hearing aids and would love for the volume of the world to be lowered just a bit.

Taken together, the effects of caffeine are not surprising, because caffeine affects all three of those aspects of introversion. It sounds like exactly the sensation that introverts attempt to avoid on a daily basis. Consider that their normal level of functioning is relatively high-strung and alert. They are already feeling the effects of two cups of caffeine without drinking any! Caffeine is one of the substances that will, in theory, push them over the edge and make them feel overwhelmed and tired instead of boosting alertness.

Feeding an introvert an excess of caffeine would be like subjecting them to an hour-long conversation. It pushes their buttons in the wrong way and just might cause them to shut down or at least become more inefficient and fatigued.

Stimulation throws introverts off, whatever the form. From that, we can extrapolate that caffeine and other stimulants are detrimental, while sedatives might be highly pleasurable. At least this theory might save you some money through buying less coffee.

Types of Introverts

Professor Jonathan Cheek of Wellesley College has broken introverts down into four distinct categories. This is another opportunity to discover more about yourself and feel less like an alien whom no one understands. Like the terms introverted extrovert or vice versa, they might all be different ways of ultimately saying the same thing; but it can help bring clarity to how you approach yourself and the world. They are all reasons that might help you understand why you are less social than others might be.

The social introvert is social but in an introverted way. They enjoy people, but in limited quantities and ways. This is closest to the traditional definition of introversion, which depends on a social battery that is ticking down faster than is desirable. For instance, they might prefer to spend time with one or two people versus attend a party. They might also prefer to spend time alone, but not because they are shy or anxious. They interact with people but have strict limits.

The thinking introvert is the type of person who is truly inward-focused. They are introspective, analytical, and thoughtful internally without having to interact with others. They're not antisocial or anxious; they might not even be constrained by their social battery. They just prefer to spend time with their own imagination and sense of creativity. The interesting part of their life is what happens in their head, not in their environment. They interact with people less because they'd rather be constructing something inside their head. Picture a habitual daydreamer; how can real life ever compare?

The anxious introvert has a bad reputation. One of the biggest misconceptions is that most introverts are this type—shy, awkward, self-conscious, and possessing low self-confidence. Of course, this creates a vicious cycle because once you are anxious, you perform worse, which invites more anxiety. Once the belief begins, it can be hard to battle out of. They don't interact with people because doing so makes them anxious, and they aren't comfortable or confident with themselves. They'll worry over what to say, feel self-conscious saying it, and then beat themselves up after the fact for making a bad impression.

The restrained introvert doesn't necessarily avoid social situations; they just tend to live at a slower pace. Therefore, big parties or concerts aren't necessarily what they enjoy. They live slowly yet think the entire time before acting. They don't interact with people because they would rather live at a relaxed pace instead of subjecting themselves to new experiences. Imagine that they are a muscle that takes a long time to warm up, so they stick to situations that cater to this speed of interaction.

Do any of these resonate with you? Just because there are four categories doesn't mean you need to fit neatly into any of them or that you can't be a mixture of all of them.

Narcissism

Most of the typical adjectives describing introverts paint the picture of someone who is reserved yet thoughtful and measured. This can be true, but the fact that someone thinks and analyzes doesn't necessarily mean that they are automatically intelligent and perceptive.

However, because of this introverted tendency, there appears to be a growing overlap between introverts and those who feel a sense of superiority over others.

It's accurate to call yourself an introvert if you get tired of people more quickly but still like them. Remember, introversion only measures your social capacity, not your aptitude or fondness of people. However, many people have started to assign themselves the label of introvert because they believe they are superior to others. In other words, the label of introvert can act as a disguise for *covert narcissists* trying to put a socially acceptable label on themselves (Preston Ni).

Narcissists and introverts might be similar at first glance, but they arrive at that point through completely different paths. Both personality types are focused, analytical, and inward-focused. However, narcissists believe that what is happening inside their heads is special and unique, and that's the reason they are inward-focused. Introverts are simply inward-focused because that's how they're biologically wired.

You may have come across someone who has labeled themselves as an introvert just so they can call themselves introspective and analytical while also demeaning other people. Here are a few specific traits of this covert narcissist.

They are judgmental and dismissive of other people. This clearly means they hold themselves in higher regard or to a higher standard than they hold others. They think they are smarter, better, or more insightful, and they are overly critical of others. In other words, they have a superiority complex to the extent that they are what psychiatrist Glen Gabbard deems "exquisitely sensitive" and handle criticism extremely poorly. That's what happens when you don't feel that you can do any wrong.

They are self-absorbed to the point that if it's not about them, they are not interested. You can see how some people might label themselves as an introvert if they are simply self-absorbed—they feel they grow tired of social interaction, when in reality, they aren't interested in social interaction when the spotlight is on other people. They demand the spotlight and feel that others are unworthy of their attention or innately lacking in value.

Finally, these covert narcissists like to classify themselves as the classic misunderstood savant. They believe they are inward-focused because their thoughts are the stuff of genius. They believe they are on a higher level of thinking than other people, so naturally they grow tired of shallow social interaction. They believe they are unique in a way that no one can understand their true value. Finally, they believe they are simply special and above other people. These beliefs lead to someone who possesses introverted traits but is truly a narcissist in hiding.

Hopefully you haven't identified with any parts of these studies! But you can see how the introvert label can be used for both good and bad these days. It can hide people's ulterior motives, it can create detrimental self-fulfilling prophecies, and yet it can help people understand their true natures effectively.

Faces as Flowers

When we think about their differences, perhaps the most common factor we use to decide whether someone's an introvert or an extrovert is how they behave, especially in social situations.

We perceive someone who easily navigates through a party and talks to every other partygoer with equally high energy as being an extrovert. On the other hand, we see someone else at that party who's hugging the wall and talking to one or two other people at most—if at all—as being an introvert. We're kind of surprised they even bother to show up at all.

We then might carry the thought through to some unreasonable assumptions about the introverts—they're "unfriendly" or "unapproachable," they're "wrapped up in themselves," or they "don't care about anybody else." Meanwhile, we might consider the extrovert as being all the good sides of that coin: "empathetic," "outgoing," "interested in everybody's lives," and so forth.

Of course, the reality is more complex. It's also possible that there's a scientific basis behind the reticence of introverts in social situations, and it has nothing to do with distaste or dislike of other human beings: there's strong evidence it's a part of their brain chemistry. Researchers at the Salk Institute for Biological Studies, led by Imma Fishman, discovered that introverts' brains may simply not be incentivized to be overly social.

Fishman's team studied 28 young adults, all of whom were assessed as being extroverts or introverts before taking part in the trials. The goal of the study was to determine whether extroverts' brains registered higher activity in response to certain stimuli than introverts. Mostly they confirmed that was true—but in the process they made an unexpected finding about introverts' brain chemistry as well.

The researchers planned to measure their subjects' responses by reading their "P300" levels. The P300 component isn't an actual physical part of the brain—it's an electronic measurement that indicates how much attention a person's brain is paying to a certain stimulus. The subjects are hooked up to electrodes and given some sort of visual, aural, or tactile stimulus. If their P300 levels are high, that means their brains are giving more attention in response to the stimulus.

Fishman broke up her subjects into separate groups, connected their heads to electronic measuring devices, and gave them all a very simple task. One group was shown sequences of pictures of human faces: 80% male faces and 20% female. They were told to press a key whenever they saw a female face. The other group was shown a picture series of flowers: 80% purple and 20% yellow. *They* were instructed to press a key whenever they saw a yellow flower.

The framework for this test is something scientists call the "oddball paradigm," and it's heavily used in experiments involving the P300 component. It's simply a test model in which subjects are given a long series of very similar stimuli interrupted by occasional, very different stimuli. The oddball paradigm is extremely effective in measuring P300 levels.

In this particular case, most of the human faces the subjects saw were men, and significantly fewer were women. Likewise, most of the flowers were purple, and far fewer were yellow. So the women and the yellow flowers were the "oddballs" (no offense intended to women or, for that matter, fans of yellow flowers). This is important to understand because of what happened in Fishman's experiments— especially among the introverts.

As expected, the extroverts' P300 levels spiked when they saw the women's faces and the yellow flowers, depending what group they were assigned. The introverts' P300 levels went up as well.

But Fishman's team discovered something else. The extroverts who viewed human faces showed higher P300 levels than extroverts who viewed the flowers across the board. But the *introverts'* P300 levels were generally the same *across the board*. To their brains, there was no significant difference in their attention levels whether they were viewing human faces *or* flowers.

The results imply that the brains of introverts, *chemically*, are not particularly "grabbed" by human faces above other stimuli, like flowers. Extroverts' P300 levels were far more active with humans. But the introverts' brains didn't register a significant difference between the two.

The findings point to the idea that introverts are therefore simply not incentivized to be social. It's not necessarily a value judgment on their part—it isn't a conscious and firmly held feeling that they don't like or mistrust other people. It's a trait of their brains, which chemically just don't find people to be a bigger deal than flowers.

What does it mean? That introverts are not inevitably resistant to social activities by choice or by emotional mandate—it's likely a neural response network that operates differently in introverts than in extroverts, that the shyness or distance many perceive in introverts may simply be because of how their brains are structured. We learned in an earlier chapter that introverts are better at analyzing and reading people's emotions, so how can these two propositions fit together? Perhaps it's because introverts can indeed analyze situations better in general but don't attach special meaning to people. In any case, this is a compelling argument for why introverts are less incentivized to be around other people.

Introverted Language Choice

Introverts and extroverts are judged to view the world differently. It's not always clear *how* exactly, but the idea is that they have varied perceptions of what they encounter or experience in the world. While there may be some truth to that, there's solid evidence that there's a big difference in how introverts and extroverts *explain* what they see.

A Dutch communications professor Camiel Beukeboom ran an experiment with 40 employees at a company in Amsterdam. Each employee was shown five different pictures of people in somewhat indefinite social situations. They were then asked to describe what they saw, with the understanding that there weren't any correct or incorrect answers. Three days after giving their responses, they finished personality quizzes that determined whether each participant leaned extrovert or introvert.

When the Beukeboom and his team reviewed the responses, they found an interesting disparity between how extroverts and introverts described the pictures. Extroverts tended to be a little more abstract in their summaries. Their reflections were more like interpretations of the scenes they saw; they made certain assumptions of the people in the photograph that weren't necessarily provable (for example, "Hans loves Emma"). They described things that weren't even evident in the photos.

Introverts, on the other hand, described the more tangible elements of the pictures. They were very precise about what they saw. They used more numbers in their descriptions ("There are four men in suits") and assessed what they actually *saw* in the photographs ("That woman is sitting separately from the other women"). They also, interestingly, used more articles like "a" and "the" than extroverts did.

The takeaway from Beukeboom's experiment was that introverts tended to be more concrete and cautious in their explanations, while extroverts were more vague and speculative. Introverts made more exact descriptions of the behaviors and elements they saw in the photos, while extroverts made more assumptions based on the personalities they projected onto the human subjects.

The introverts were also more inclined to state that the behaviors and activities of the people in the photos were probably specific to the situation they were in—for example, they seemed to be more upbeat because they were in a party atmosphere.

Meanwhile, extroverts thought the behaviors the people showed were more likely to recur in different situations simply because of their *personalities*.

It's a little tricky to explain the ramifications of this study without sounding critical of one group over the other. But one possible interpretation of the results is that introverts are more concrete and realistic in their language. The explanation of introverts' descriptions tends to be more reliable and easily verified. On the other hand, extroverts' descriptions tend to be more critical and less confirmable. This would fall in line with the general thoughtfulness and judgmental character of introverts. They can make assumptions because they are more likely to be well-founded or at least thoughtful.

This *does not mean* extroverts are deluded and don't see the truth about situations. There is great value in speculation and interpretation. And let's face it, speculation is often *right*.

But it *does* mean introverts are likely to make decisions based only on what they can see and substantiate—they're less likely to assume things that aren't there. That can be of great value. If an introvert stumbles upon a confusing or threatening situation, they may be more likely to maintain a level head and navigate through it with more attention to the here and now. This provides another factor for why introverts might be less interested in other people— they know the potential discomfort and displeasure they will face, and so they avoid it. Extroverts, on the other hand, are vaguer about what lies ahead, which can actually be empowering for some instead of prone to invoking fear.

Overall, language is always an intentional choice, and the difference likely reflects the difference in how the world presents itself. One perspective is black and white, while the other is far more flexible and forgiving.

Takeaways:

- Though it is the topic of this book, this chapter in particular presents introverts from a broad perspective. Through the lens of the most recent research, we learn quite a bit more about introverts than the fact that their social batteries are king.

- Introverts are more judgmental than extroverts because of how much they live inside their heads and think. Naturally, they think everyone else should act like this when it's not true.

- Introverts should be wary of caffeine because it simulates the type of stimulation that can overwhelm a social battery.

- There are four different types of introverts: social, anxious, restrained, and thinking.

- Introverts and covert narcissists share many of the same traits, though they end up there through completely different means. But still, there might be an overlap between the two populations.

- Introverts have been shown to literally not be able to distinguish faces from flowers. This is a peek into how they perceive and value social situations.

- Introverts use more concrete, judgmental, and intentional language, while extroverts are slower to judge, more flexible, and more open to interpretation.

Chapter 5. Temperamental Relationships

One of the more interesting areas of study in personality and temperament is surrounding relationships—what happens when opposites come together and how does it work out? Can we find some sort of formula for successful relationships based on personality traits? Are humans so simple and predictable as to be reduced to five traits (OCEAN)?

You might feel this is the *most* compelling of all topics involving personality. Relationships, platonic or romantic, are what drive us and color our days, whether we like it or not. They have the power to instantly brighten up our days or flush them down the toilet. Countless books are written about not just dating, but also relationships, each year.

So do opposites attract, or do birds of a feather flock together? As a caveat, do opposites attract and *then* attack? Is too much of the same simply redundant and bound to clash? Should we seek complementary mates?

In other words, what role does personality play in successful relationships, romantic and otherwise? Are introverts and extroverts better off dating people with similar personality types, or can they benefit more from being with somebody who has a different perspective and lifestyle? Is there really definitive knowledge on this, or is this chapter just going to be an analysis of assumptions and logic? Well, both.

But let's be honest—what we really want to know is which scenarios have the highest probability of success and happiness and which ones are more likely to cause distress and dissatisfaction. That's okay—me too, and that's why I included this chapter.

It's first important to call attention to research regarding introverts and perception.

While introverts are thought to be reluctant to mix in extended social circles and spend a lot of time within their own thoughts, that doesn't mean they have no insight into the lives of others. In fact, science suggests that they know more about the workings of other people than you might think.

Yale scientists Anton Gollwitzer and John Bargh interviewed over 1,000 subjects about how people felt, thought, and acted in social situations. They sought to find out if individual differences were prevalent and whether a person's psychological makeup made them more likely to judge social behaviors accurately or engage in self-deception to stay relevant in public situations.

Gollwitzer and Bargh found that introverts, lonely people, and those suffering from self-esteem issues were more apt to answer the questions accurately. In addition to being remarkably skilled at the act of introspection, they showed almost no motivational biases. The scientists theorized that was because they spent a lot of time observing others and formulating perceptions that were more on the mark.

Gollwitzer even said that introverts' skills at analyzing others in the social group rivals, if not equals, the skills of professional psychologists: "These results raise the striking possibility that certain individuals can predict the accuracy of unexplored social psychological phenomena better than others. Society could potentially harness individuals' accuracy at inferring social psychological phenomena for beneficial means. Mastering social psychological principles, for example, may help us anticipate mass panics, political movements, and societal and cultural changes."

The research would appear to convey that though extroverts are more comfortable existing and moving in the outside world, introverts might have the upper hand when it comes to reading people—a handy skill in relationships, to say the least. This could correlate with their own habits toward intense self-analysis: if introverts recognize and question their own motivations with depth and direction, then perhaps they can do so with others.

This skill might not actually help in relationships with clashing personalities, but it's sometimes important to know that even though the introvert doesn't say anything, they are definitely *watching*.

Mixed-Personality Relationships

At the core of the differences between extroverts and introverts in relationships, we end up with one common dilemma.

The extrovert wants to go out and recharge their social battery while doing so has the opposite effect on the introvert, who would rather stay in and re-energize in the peace and quiet of their home. The extrovert also constantly wants to interact and spend time with the introvert, who needs solitude from time to time. Think of the difference between a golden retriever and a fickle cat, where the golden retriever keeps wanting to snuggle up or play while the cat just wants to glare at the dog in peace.

Considering that these opposite perspectives determine how a significant portion of the time couples are together will be spent, it's worth taking a deeper look.

It's important to know each other's limits and motivations. For extroverts, how much time can they spend at home alone or with their introverted partner—watching TV together, sharing a meal, or maybe even not interacting at all? And for the introvert in the relationship, how much socializing is enjoyable or at least manageable before it becomes exhausting and overwhelming? If a romantic relationship is about companionship, what are the needs for each partner?

We learned in an earlier chapter that exhibiting extroverted behavioral tendencies—even if you are an introvert—

can lead to greater feelings of happiness. So for introverts who otherwise lack the motivation to simply "show up" to many of the social gatherings available to them, having an extroverted partner to draw them out of their shell can actually be a boon. In this case, the two personalities can complement each other, though not all the time.

Not only does spending more time with a loved one, or even a casual romantic interest, provide an incentive for introverts to go out more, but this can make the interactions themselves less taxing on their limited social energy.

While together, the extroverted partner in the relationship can do the brunt of the socializing and take any undesired attention away from the introvert while also providing comfort and stability, enabling the introvert to feel more relaxed and confident in social situations than they typically do.

In this case, the extrovert gets the social energy they need while the introvert has more positive feelings about the interaction than they usually do. The opposite scenario can also be mutually beneficial—if the introverted partner gets to decide the agenda, leaving the extrovert to their own imagination and allowing them to focus and get rid of distractions. It's a win-win.

That's not to say that these extrovert/introvert relationships can succeed if only the introvert becomes more extroverted or the extrovert becomes more introverted. In fact, such a one-sided compromise will almost surely create resentment in the end. That's how people end up performing pale imitations of other people.

The key here is balance. Achieving the proper balance means that the introvert has enough downtime to feel energized and recharge or to make social occasions as easy as possible for them; the extrovert has enough social interaction to feel energized, whether they get it from their partner or someone else; *and* nobody's feelings get hurt along the way. The last part is the crux of the matter in navigating these relationships.

Both members of the relationship need to understand their partner's needs and not take it personally when those needs don't align with what they want. It's not a slight when the introvert doesn't want to attend that office holiday party with their extroverted partner's coworkers, who they barely know, just as it's not a slight when the extrovert decides to spend a night out socializing with friends instead of watching a movie at home.

To make a clearer illustration, imagine someone who is sensitive to the sun and burns easily and someone who needs the sun for their health. They are a couple. How might they create a compromise that takes care of their needs, even though they seem to be at odds with one another? Mostly, it requires some empathy and understanding of separate needs.

"I love you. I just don't want to see you right now, and that's okay" is something that is the unspoken mode of operating. Both partners need to feel that they can responsibly manage their own social needs without hurting the other's feelings.

This may all sound easy in principle, but putting it into practice when introducing other complex variables can make things tricky—for instance, when you deal with anxiety, stress, insecurity, or jealousy. Is there a way to kill two birds with one stone and feed both people's needs?

Introverts are less likely to enjoy spending hours at a crowded event and extroverts may be prone to boredom in situations with lower social requirements or stimulation. What's the healthy medium?

Boil down what each partner is actually looking for. If introverts are to be social, there must be a purpose other than socializing for socialization's sake, because that grows tiresome sooner rather than later. Thus, introverts have to find alternative value in a social activity. Extroverts are interested in interaction and being around people. There's plenty of overlap to find a happy medium or compromise when you look at it that way. This is easily found in social hobbies.

Compromises can range from browsing stores, exploring interesting areas, traveling together, playing video games with or against each other, going to the movie theater instead of watching movies at home, or even pursuing different interests while still enjoying each other's presence in the same physical space. Just make sure there is always a social aspect, as well as an activity or interest to focus on otherwise. There are so many ways that couples with one introvert and one extrovert can spend plenty of time together while both having their needs fulfilled.

And it is often in these happy-medium activities that the contrasting personality types can really complement each other. Let's take traveling as an example.

The introvert in the relationship may enjoy planning the details of the trip: booking affordable airfare, reading through reviews to find the perfect accommodations, etc. Upon arrival at the destination, the extrovert can take social pressure off of the introvert—making comfortable small talk with the taxi driver or approaching strangers in the hope of making new friends to share the adventures with, to name just a couple examples.

In this way, the travel experience can be better for both partners, as they get to spend more time doing the things they enjoy while their partner happily does the activities that the other partner considers less desirable.

In order to get the greatest benefit from your relationship, being open-minded and willing to leave your comfort zone can go a long way. Being with your partner and learning about them provides a fantastic opportunity for your own personal development, exposing you to new ideas and ways of thinking that can improve upon your own.

Mixed-personality relationships just might have the highest potential for benefiting both partners. While sharing many personality traits can certainly make a relationship easier, it's the differences that might make it so much more interesting and valuable for your life. Expect that it will be difficult at times and require ongoing effort and communication, but it is certainly possible to navigate these challenging situations successfully.

Overall, a complementary partner can allow you to do what you do best and not worry about what you hate—if you don't kill each other first.

Aside from how to deal with the different needs of partners, another important issue in relationships is how stress and negativity are handled. Even the happiest of relationships hit setbacks and misunderstandings from time to time, and they need to be dealt with. Just by temperament alone, you might assume that introverts are less willing to seek confrontation or social support during times of stress. This is an issue of communication more than anything else.

It's true that introverts have a natural tendency to internalize more—positive and negative—so they might bottle things up inside or find other outlets for their negativity in an attempt to avoid what is seen as unnecessary confrontation or simply to preserve their limited social battery. Stress can't grow indefinitely, so it's possible this might lead to volcanic eruptions when a certain threshold is reached.

Extroverts will likely need to pry a bit and lead their introverted partner if they wish to have more open communication. This can be unpleasant for both sides, especially if the extrovert is prone to avoiding conflict. Remember, just because you seek social interaction doesn't mean you seek all types of it.

For many introverts, the internalization of emotions may be a result of having the mindset that such matters are personal and that nobody else would really care or want to know about them. That, or they are socially fatigued just thinking about it and thus keep it inside. As an extrovert, continuously expressing a desire to provide emotional support and have open communication—while still being perceptive of how your partner responds to it and not badgering the issue when they seem unreceptive—can gradually lead to a healthier relationship.

In 2010, Australian psychologist John Malouff and colleagues examined the findings of 10 studies—involving nearly 3,900 total participants—which had been conducted on personality and relationship satisfaction among heterosexual partners.

These studies found that introverts had lower levels of satisfaction than more extroverted partners. These findings held true even when the research team considered the possibility that introverts might be more likely to marry other introverts, thus inflating the apparent correlation between personality type and happiness.

It could also just be an extension of the previous chapter, in which we learned that extroverts are generally in a better state of mental well-being because they either place themselves into happiness's way more frequently or perceive negativity differently than introverts. Perhaps introverts are generally just more malcontented by nature, which is not necessarily negative.

But being in close proximity with another human being introduces a host of other potential issues. It's basically impossible to isolate the personality dimension of extroversion/introversion from other attributes such as conscientiousness, neuroticism—the tendency to be anxious or worried—and openness to new experiences. For as comprehensive as the Australian research team's study was, it failed to examine the full spectrum of personality traits as they related to introversion.

One idea this study supports is that it might be easier to be in a relationship with somebody similar to you. The more similarities shared, the better mutual understanding there will naturally be. This is especially important during times of stress and anger, when it can be the difference between constant misunderstanding and instant commiseration. Is too much similarity ever bad? You can imagine a pair of extroverts locked in a self-perpetuating recharging cycle like an extension plug that plugs into itself.

The question you can ask yourself here is this: what do you want from your relationships? It's certainly nice to have relationships that just work naturally without tons of effort required—but then again, will such relationships provide the same potential for personal growth and learning as ones with partners who contrast?

In the end, our ideal match on paper rarely seems to align with the people in real life that we find ourselves most attracted to as a relationship partner, so we can take solace in the knowledge that there are some definite positives to having matches from across the personality continuum. In other words, whatever laundry list of requirements and preferences you write up for yourself will probably be obliterated by the person you actually fall for anyway. But it's nice and occasionally productive to think about.

The Beast with Two Backs

We couldn't very well have a chapter about relationships without mentioning sex, could we? Sex is one of the fundamental forces driving human behavior, regardless of position on the extrovert/introvert continuum or various other personality traits, and it can play a very crucial role in the success or failure of a relationship.

A large study conducted in West Germany gave university students a standard personality test called the Eysenck Personality Inventory (EPI) to categorize participants, and then it asked them about their level of sexual activity.

Extroverted men reported having sex 5.5 times a month on average, compared to three times per month for introverted men. Extroverted women were the most sexually active, reporting having sex 7.5 times per month on average, compared to 3.1 times per month for introverted women.

Before discussing these results further, there is a caveat worth mentioning—this study was self-reported, leaving open the ever so small possibility for people to be dishonest and thus the data to be inaccurate.

But even if extroverts inflated their numbers, based on the discrepancy between extroverts and introverts of both genders, it seems safe to conclude that extroverts are in fact having more sex than introverts. So it is our goal to determine what factors are actually causing extroverts to have more sex and what conclusions we can draw from this information.

Given the scope of this study, it would be irresponsible to stretch the data into any conclusions about extroverts being more sexual—or having higher libidos—than introverts. It is more reasonable to explain the results with what we do know for a fact about extroverts, which is that they are more motivated to place themselves in social situations frequently, to interact with more people, and to seek company more often. All of those behaviors associated with extroversion lead to a higher volume of opportunities to interact with potential sexual partners, which will increase the probability of sex occurring.

Considering that extroverts are more likely to place themselves in social situations also implies that extroverts are more likely to meet other extroverts in such situations. So not only are extroverts meeting more potential partners than introverts, but those partners are also generally more likely to be extroverted, furthering the trend of extroverts having more sex. This makes a lot of sense. Where an introvert might stay home from a party, the extrovert would attend and stay until the wee hours of the morning, connecting for hours with someone new. Doesn't sound like an introvert's cup of tea, at least not at the outset.

Add in the knowledge that introverts are more likely to have neurotic characteristics—experiencing anxiety or nervousness in social situations—and we have even more reason to believe that the amount of sex people are having is more driven by personality and social factors than actual sex drive.

Let's compare two examples.

First, we have two extroverts in a relationship, both with similarly high sex drives. There are good odds that they will have a healthy amount of sex that makes both of them happy because they will be willing to communicate and express desires and emotions openly with one another.

They enjoy spending a massive amount of time together, which we can probably say will increase the chances for sex.

Now, let's contrast that with a relationship consisting of two introverts, also both having similarly high sex drives. While it's entirely possible they will likewise be having the healthy amount of sex that they each desire, there are simply so many more potential obstacles to overcome in reaching that point.

These include wanting more alone time or being more tired as a result of social interaction, thus not being in the mood for sex; experiencing negative emotions and not expressing them openly to one another, thus not being in the mood for sex; having anxiety about what their partner is thinking because they don't communicate openly, leading to possible self-esteem and confidence issues and thus not being in the mood for sex—you get the point.

Once again, it's not that the ideal is unattainable for introverts; it simply may require more effort and commitment to get there.

So what are the implications for mixed-personality relationships?

You can be friends or acquaintances with anyone, but if you are spending 90% of your free time with a partner, there will inevitably be complications and quirks to deal with. This is inescapable for even the most understanding and empathetic of couples. Sometimes you'll feel like you are two puzzle pieces that fit together perfectly, and other times you'll feel like a cat and dog trying to mate.

As in all types of relationships, similar sexual libido helps a lot. Regardless of personality type, if one partner desires constant sexual activity and the other couldn't care less about it, that will almost certainly cause all kinds of problems. On the other hand, if the two individuals of a mixed-personality couple have similar sex drives, other factors such as open communication, openness to new experiences, confidence, and comfort with each other will greatly determine the satisfaction each feels about their sex life.

We know from the previous chapter that people can indeed change; it just takes a plan, powerful motivation, and persistence. It's possible to change our behaviors and personalities to adapt to a partner to a reasonable extent. Ultimately, it may depend on your capacity and appetite for growth and challenge. Whether we should or not is an entirely different issue.

Leader Material

Not all relationships have to be romantic or even friendly by nature. What about the relationships in our careers and with coworkers? How does our personality impact us there? This is best discussed in the context of leadership.

There is a long-standing belief that an outgoing personality is more effective as a leader or manager. Extroverts used to be pictured as the big bosses who could command a room and inspire a company.

Naturally, we imagine leaders to be people who inspire with the sound of their voices like Martin Luther King Jr. It seems that those who rise to visibility in most contexts appear to be extroverts.

In 2009, clinical researchers Deniz Ones and Stephan Dilchert published a study in the journal *Industrial and Organizational Psychology*. Results of that study showed that 96% of leaders and managers reported being extroverted. They also discovered that those executives felt that only 6% saw introversion as an advantage for corporate leaders.

Does that stereotype hold true? Is our conception of leadership based on what we *think* will work versus what works in real life?

In the 21st-century world, the reign of the pure extrovert as the only type of leader desired is over. Extroversion is not necessarily a good quality in a leader. It depends on the purpose, the employees, and the situation.

In a 2010 study, Adam Grant, Francesco Gina, and David A. Hoffman researched the issue of personality type (extroverted/introverted) for effectiveness in leadership positions. For their first study, they tested this out by conducting a field study of 130 pizza delivery franchises in a high-volume college town.

Results showed that extroverted leaders were more effective in terms of profitability as opposed to introverted leaders. Why was this, and was it restricted to the pizza delivery context?

Grant and company found that oftentimes a business needs someone who is quick-thinking and who can act instinctively. Extroverted leaders do not hesitate in favor of analyzing a situation. They don't shy away from others because they don't get exhausted by them. These types of leader work well in a highly demanding, fast-paced field like a franchise operation as described in the study. Imagine that working in a busy environment is like a pressure cooker with no room for breaks or recharging of a social battery. This is the extrovert's home territory.

Extroverted leaders have great strengths, especially in stressful and aggressive work environments where communication and speed are paramount. What's more, they can help the more passive and quiet among their workers become enthusiastic. Extroverted leaders themselves exude enthusiasm, and it spreads to their employees as well.

At first glance, you may give an extroverted leader a higher satisfaction rating. However, that may not be true universally. It still depends.

One of the weaknesses of the extroverted leader is the fact that he or she might feel more threatened by strongly motivated employees. The leader may feel that his or her position is being challenged and that the very proactive, very self-directed employees might attract a great deal of interest and attention by business owners.

As a result, extroverted leaders may discourage motivated workers and those who are very proactive. In order to compensate, they may change a company's atmosphere into one of subservience, fear, and even frustration.

While the assertiveness of extroverted leaders is good, they may miss out on any new and creative ideas their employees might have. When it comes to effective management, the extroverted leader may fail to maximize the group's actual productivity. This can take the form of too much distractibility or even constant micromanaging.

Nate G. was a good example of an extroverted leader. He was the head of the collection department at an interstate bank. Nate established a viable system of incentives for his collectors. They were rewarded monthly when they successfully reached their goals. That resulted in an offset for the debts incurred by the bank. His dogged insistence that his workers meet their goals was one of Nate's greatest strengths.

But he had a weakness: his employees were afraid of him! They tried to duck behind their computer screens whenever he walked the floor. The turnover rate for that department was high because many employees quit due to anxiety. Eventually the bank started to suffer a loss because they had to keep training new workers in the collection department.

If you are a leader, or plan on becoming one, are you extroverted in terms of your personality style? Of course, you want to be aware of your strengths. However, are you insightful about the possible pitfalls of being primarily an extrovert?

In their follow-up study, Grant et al. recruited 163 college students. The students' main task was to get as many T-shirts folded in 10 minutes as they possibly could. The researchers then introduced another variable: passivity/proactivity among the participants. They then split the group into two sections: passive members and proactive members. Passive members had extroverted leaders. Proactive members, on the other hand, had introverted leaders.

The introverted leaders coached the participants to use their own innovative techniques to get the job done faster. The results of this study were entirely different than the results from the earlier study. The proactive group led by introverted leaders folded 28% more T-shirts than those with extroverted leaders.

For this second study, the introverted leaders permitted the students to participate in the accomplishment of the task. They listened to the participants and showed that they valued their input. They permitted the participants to assist in task accomplishment. In this study, the introverted leaders excelled in leadership.

Sometimes, introverted leaders are better, and it depends entirely on the context and task at hand.

They can draw the most out of the employees who work for them. Those employees can be type-A personalities who are ambitious, highly-motivated, and outcome-driven. They make the company goals their goals. It is an ideal situation when the leaders and the employees all work together to make a company profitable. It also brings the workers a sense of personal satisfaction and self-esteem. Introverted leaders are typically better listeners, which is the preferred way of social interaction in this kind of work environment. It is also less tiring and allows these introverted leaders more time and energy to focus on the work at hand.

If you are an introverted leader, there are drawbacks if you let your introversion get out of hand. While it is true that you need some "down" time, your first instinct may be to go into your office and shut the door. Perhaps you might even put your headphones on and turn up the music. If that happens, you might send out signals to your employees that you do not invite their input. In addition, you might inadvertently create office gossip, which takes time away from the work priorities of the day.

Ted T. was your proverbial introverted leader. He was appointed head of the auto sales department at a large dealership. He coached his salespeople by teaching them how to listen to potential customers' concerns. He coached them to come up with ideas of their own and always kept in mind the budgetary limitations of the new customers. New car sales tripled from what they were before Ted became sales manager. However, his weakness did hurt him. Sometimes Ted wandered the sales yard and his employees couldn't find him when they needed his input. This created a lot of office gossip. His workers would gather in groups and talk about him behind his back. Ted, as a result, lost the respect of some of his sales staff.

If you tend toward introversion, it is important to note your strengths and maximize them. However, are you aware of some of the weaknesses that might affect you and your staff? It is helpful to know that some of the perennial tendencies of the introvert may demoralize you and discourage you from the success you crave and deserve.

In his 2013 article for *Psychological Science*, Adam Grant, infamous for his research on extroversion and introversion in leadership, conducted a study of leaders of sales at a software company. For this study, he considered three types of subjects: the extroverted, the introverted, and the ambiverted. Ambiverts have developed the ability to slide from the extroverted style of leadership to the introverted style. Results of the study were astonishing. Grant discovered that the introverted group made the least amount of money, the extroverted group made slightly more money, but the ambiverts made the most!

In conclusion, Grant said, "Ambiverts achieve greater sales productivity than extroverts or introverts do. Because they naturally engage in a flexible pattern of talking and listening, ambiverts are likely to express sufficient assertiveness and enthusiasm to persuade and close a sale but are more inclined to listen to customers' interests and less vulnerable to appearing too excited or overconfident."

A leader requires the ability to adapt. Leaders do not have the luxury of retreating into their introverted or extroverted comfort zones. Instead, they must be "ambiverts" and have a flexible attitude depending upon the situation. In his article for the *Washington Post,* Daniel Pink, a business writer and consultant, has said, "They're not quiet, but they're not loud. They know how to assert themselves, but they're not pushy."

In light of all the competition in today's marketplace, do you remain open to all the challenges you might face? Once you know if you are more of an extrovert or more of an introvert, are you courageous enough to be flexible? Although it may be uncomfortable to change your pattern, just think about the satisfaction you'll experience if you could shift from extroversion to introversion to meet the particular situations that you will face.

Leadership encompasses listening, caring, validating concerns, and soliciting employee participation. Leadership also includes getting others to listen to your visions, follow your direction, and be productive for your companies. Both the extroverted and the introverted leaders can succeed, depending on the field of work, employee interest levels and skills, work environment, and mustering employee support. Both types of leaders have their distinctive strengths and weaknesses.

The ambivert style of leaders has the ability to move from one end of the spectrum (extroverted) to the other (introverted). This is an ideal situation, but it does represent a non-static, fluid, and flexible condition. This state is sometimes achieved, but sometimes it is not. We deal with a reality that is fallible at best.

Are you an ambivert? Surely throughout your life you have been able to act in an extroverted capacity and in an introverted role as well. You have led others in some social interactions. You have benefited from time to yourself to reflect and gain insight into your work habits and your life. That includes all that you are and all that you will be in the days to come. The most important factor, above all, is your ability to "change channels." That means that you can slide from one end of the range to the other easily and carefully. Even back home in your family environment, you want to be both a parent who is loving and open to your children *and* a parent who must function as a disciplinarian at times. This balance and flexibility is difficult to achieve.

Takeaways:

- Interpersonal relationships are the root of why we discuss introversion and extroversion, for the most part. We want to understand ourselves and the people around us better to increase the happiness and fulfillment of everyone's lives. That's my optimistic interpretation, anyway. So what dynamics exist in the context of personality and temperament?

- What happens when an introvert and extrovert become partners? Compromise is paramount because what each partner values, the other expressly does not want. A key here is to focus on social hobbies—shared activities with a social aspect and an activity or interest-based aspect. However, it can also be said that these two personalities can complement and bring out the best in each other, compensating for perceived shortcomings and allowing each partner to focus on what they do best. It all depends.
- The overall lower happiness levels experienced by introverts also carry over into relationships.
- When it comes to sex, extroverts definitively have more of it. Is this because they place themselves into more situations with the possibility for sex and the law of probability works in their favor or because they have higher libidos in general? Probably the former.

- Finally, when it comes to leadership, the answer again becomes "it depends." Extroverted leaders can excel when there is stress and in close quarters with employees, but introverts appear to be better at drawing more out of people and giving them the space they need to succeed. The best, as with everything, is probably a mixture, embodied by the ambivert—which we all are, anyway.

Chapter 6. Introvert Action Plan

Yes, this is a book about personality type. However, it's also a book that wants to help people understand themselves and socialize better. Therefore, this final chapter is about tips for introverts to manage their social batteries better.

For the introvert, what happens when they can't steal away from others when their social batteries have run out? Suppose they have two more events to attend that same day—what is one to do? This is where strategic management becomes important, and this book is more than a field guide to who you are. It's a field guide to improving your presence.

Categorize and Plan Interaction

In designing your life's interactions, you first have to understand the different types of social interactions there are and how they might affect your social battery. Some of these immediately sound off-putting and like a nightmare to you, while others you might think, "Yeah, I could do that frequently." Obviously, the goal is to skew your life toward more of the latter situations. This is entirely within our control.

For our purposes, you can divide social interactions into four main categories, from most dreaded to most desired. You can plan your days and weeks by how tiring these events are.

Category never: mostly strangers. These are what we typically hate because there is so much uncertainty and background chatter. It's tough to focus on one person because there is so much going on. There's no agenda and no sense of predictability. Of course, these are networking events, huge parties, and music festivals where you aren't excited about the musical acts. Plainly put, these are nightmares that you try to avoid every time but aren't always able to do so. They are exhausting and can cause you to withdraw for days afterward. You might not even make it all the way through and just leave in the middle of any of these. Tolerance: 1–3 hours.

Category occasional: lots of familiar faces. This differs from the first category because even though there are many people, you know or at least recognize almost all of them. This situation is still tiring, but nowhere near as tiring as having to break down barriers with each new stranger. Some of these faces might be annoying and fatiguing, but others will likely be sources of comfort and refuge. Friends or not, it's just a lot of stimulation and you'll still be exhausted by the end of it. This can even be your own birthday party where you handpicked every single person. Tolerance: 2–4 hours.

Category unavoidable: daily life. This is a variable category and can reach across the other three categories. Most of the time, it's simply the amount of interaction you get from your job, school, buying things, intermittent chatting, and meeting with friends. If you stop to have a chat with a barista or cashier a few times a day, you might be more tired than usual, but you'll still have to get through class, a work meeting, and chatting with a professor.

Sometimes you'll be able to stick to a routine where nothing drains you. All these seemingly small things take up bits of your social battery. Your state of mind and general state of fatigue or energy also affect how daily life affects you. In any case, you'll constantly be draining slowly. This is what causes us to, immediately after we get home from work, yank our pants off and lie comatose on the couch for a few minutes. Tolerance: 6–10 hours.

Category acceptable: immune people. Everyone has safe people with whom they actually don't really drain and with whom they feel absolute safety. For some, this will be their significant others. For others, this will be a small handful of family or friends. Some might only have one person in this category! What makes these people immune is a certain threshold of comfort and the fact that we feel they accept our introverted tendencies. They seem to understand us and our nature and don't demand that we are any other way but ourselves. Also, we can spend time together for companionship without much actual socialization. Whether it's them or us, they don't drain us. Tolerance: almost infinite.

It's time to ask yourself who falls into these categories and whether you need to start regulating or limiting some of them. Take a moment to dissect your life and place people where they need to be for your own sanity. When you can generally understand the categories of interaction that you'll be facing in a given day, you can better design your life around conserving your energy and never causing what might be deemed *the irritating of the introvert.*

A similar concept to categorizing your interactions is to expressly plan around your energy expenditure.

If you're like most people, you probably plan your schedule and calendar around your *availability*. For example, if you're free both Saturday afternoon and evening, then you would fill it with two activities. You're not taking anything into consideration other than how many hours you have free that are not accounted for.

This is not a smart thing for introverts to do.

Introverts should plan around *energy expenditure*. Let's assume that an introvert has 100 energy units a day. How will you use them to your greatest benefit? Suppose that your Saturday afternoon plans consume 60 energy units and your Saturday night plans consume 70 energy units. You obviously can't do both—or at least it would be extremely unwise of you.

What do you do? Skip one and focus on the other, attend one and only part of the other, or skip both and substitute something that consumes fewer energy units. You should have checked your energy expenditure instead of openings in your schedule.

Planning around the expected expenditure and not your time availability is going to help you budget your energy better so you don't get overwhelmed, because you manage yourself better and don't place yourself in situations to get overwhelmed. Understand your own boundaries and, like the previous point, gain a conscious understanding of what you have been doing to yourself.

If you complain about always being socially exhausted, you might be doing it to yourself without realizing it. Just because your time is free does not mean that you should be using it.

Try to assign a rough estimate of how many energy units each activity will consume and give it an honest assessment. If you have only 100 per day, then you'll begin to see how to use them more effectively and budget your days. You can look at it like a game of Tetris with your energy that requires some creative arranging. You might also set yourself a limited number of social activities per week or weekend. Understand your limits and respect them.

If you tend to find yourself overbooked, something that may help with this is to *batch* your interactions together. This means that instead of having an activity on Thursday, Friday, and Saturday, try to collect the people you were going to see on these three separate days and put them into consecutive activities on Saturday—one right after the other.

You may not get time in between these activities, but you will get plenty of time before and afterward to charge up and recharge. In a sense, you are capitalizing on your momentum and taking care of everything at once, giving yourself larger breaks and less consistent activity. Constant activity can be far more tiring than having one day that you are a bit wary of.

With batching, you are able to create huge cushions of solitude to prepare and unwind with.

The final aspect of planning your interactions is to make sure that you can predict as much of it as possible. Of course, this helps you with categorizing them and estimating energy expenditure, but one of the aspects of random or obligatory socialization that introverts hate is the unpredictability of it all.

Events or activities that are open-ended, or that you have no knowledge about, scare the dickens out of you because, well, how long is your battery going to last, and when will you be able to recharge it?

Consider, for example, bar hopping—going with a group of people from bar to bar. Extroverts love this because the more bars they go to, the more different people they can engage with. There is action and movement, which energizes them.

The problem with socializing this way for introverts is that mixing with people and environments in unfamiliar territory requires untold amounts of social effort and attention. It's like you need to be at maximum alertness to process and comprehend everything going on around you.

When you go to these places, you don't know who will be there. You don't know if there is an agenda. And even if there is an agenda, you don't know how it can deviate and take a turn for something you are wholly unprepared for.

Therefore, one of the keys to designing your life is to focus on predictability. Think about the *who, what, when, where,* and *why*. Insist on knowing these things before you head out to any event and be intimately aware of these when you plan events for yourself. It's okay to have a little variation, but at least make sure it's variation you have accounted for! Remember, you're not actively controlling situations—you're simply filtering and understanding what you're up against.

Where. Focus on locations and settings that you know you will be comfortable in and where you know there will be few surprises. This speaks to venues and restaurants that you already know or are quiet and calm versus loud and animated. Will you be able to have a decent conversation, or is the venue conducive only to salsa dancing?

Who. Know who you will be spending time with and try to restrict the number of people to your close circle so you don't get overwhelmed talking to large groups. Restrict your socialization to just one or two strangers at a time—any more than that will be too tiring for you. Are the attendees chatterboxes, and if so, how many? Will there be people present who understand your nature and can indulge in it? Try to avoid people who spontaneously proclaim, "Hey, it's okay if I invite eight more people, right?"

When. This isn't a point about being punctual; rather, it's a point about having defined beginning and ending times. This puts a limit on the expenditure of your social battery. The most important part of this is to know exactly what you're getting yourself into time-wise and to give yourself a solid time to leave. You may not be able to count on yourself for leaving at a certain time, but if the event ends, then that can help you out. Keep it close-ended and nonnegotiable. It's for your own good.

What. This can tie neatly into the previous section about the categories of stimulation. What is the purpose of the event, what is the normal type of behavior there, and how will you be expected to act? Is the energy expenditure worth the payoff?

As mentioned, we don't mind talking while we are waiting in a grocery line or in an elevator, because we know these have defined ending points where we can escape.

Keep the same in mind for your social events and occasions—know exactly how long they will be and when you will leave. It's impossible to understand every single scenario possible, but if you can prepare yourself with alternative options, your stress will decrease because you won't feel trapped and like you have no choice but to be incredibly uncomfortable.

By chasing predictability, you make sure you are prepared for what's to come and have the proper expectations about an event or hangout *before* you get there. You can do this by asking many thorough questions, most of which are designed to help you gauge just how socially exhausting something will be.

In essence, play a game of "twenty questions" before agreeing to anything social and you will be much happier with your friends.

For example, if a friend were to invite me to "a small party," I might show up and find that his definition of "small" is 40 people, none of whom I know. I would be annoyed at myself for not having more information beforehand and trying to determine if the social cost is worth the social benefit.

It's up to you to perform your due diligence before a social outing. Get as much information as possible so you can truly determine if you're up for it, if you can *get up* for it, and if you'll enjoy it.

Questions to ask:
- When does it start and end?
- Who is going?
- How many people are going?
- Who will I know there?
- What's the occasion?
- Where will it be?
- How do I get there?
- Will there be loud music?

Knowing the answers to these questions will allow you to pace yourself for the night or just opt out.

Become a Question Master

To pace yourself for social exertion better, there are even more questions you should ask. This is because the part about interaction that drains your social battery is answering people's questions and expressing your thoughts. Telling a story or talking about your day is far more strenuous than asking about someone else's and acknowledging their answer.

Thus, asking questions of other people ranks far, far lower on how it drains your social battery. It represents a more passive role versus active role in answering questions. Think about a job interview and how much more the interviewee is expected to talk and feels the pressure— you should strive to be on the more relaxed side of the interviewer.

Become the question master. People enjoy talking about themselves and what interests them, so if you can ask questions that convey your interest in them, you will be set for a while.

When's the last time you asked someone five questions in a row? Does that feel weird or uncomfortable? If you mentally answered yes, you clearly don't ask many questions and are inadvertently putting yourself into the active role in a conversation of answering questions. You're tiring yourself out with unnecessary motion.

Try this on for size: no matter how the other person replies, you will ask them four questions. Then, after the four questions, share something about yourself. There's essentially a ratio of four to one of talking about the other person to talking about yourself. Even if you know you should ask more questions, sometimes it can be hard to think of what to ask, effectively fatiguing you and undermining the whole thing. Sometimes, we can't help but fall into interview mode where we interrogate people about shallow details in their lives. Instead of struggling with that on the fly, you can separate your questions into two types that allow you to avoid interview mode: specific and broad questions.

Specific questions are about specific details and components of a topic. If you're talking about tables, specific questions would be where you bought it, how much it cost, what the material is, why you bought this particular table, or who paid for it. You are asking for distinct pieces of information and facts. You're investigating and hunting for information as if you want to do what they did.

Broad questions are when you zoom out on a topic and try to understand the context around it. If you're talking about tables, broad questions would be the motivation for a new table, home décor, the thought process, or why the old table was inadequate. You are asking for thoughts and reasons as opposed to information and facts. You are hunting for information as if you are thinking about making a decision similar to theirs and evaluating it and performing due diligence.

Knowing that you don't necessarily have to come off as an interrogator can free you and put more conversational burden on other people. With practice, you'll see that you can elicit entire stories, backstories, and explanations from people with a simple question or even statement phrased as a question. Then all you have to do is sit back and listen.

This even works with small talk, though there is a separate way to deal specifically with that. We must begrudgingly recognize that small talk is often the path to real relationships.

The way that you might start talking to and connect with your future best friend is probably through a combination of small talk and randomized connection. No matter whom we meet, it's usually the gatekeeper that we have to get past to connect with people on a deeper level.

Most of the purpose of small talk is to aim for the lowest common denominator, the lowest hanging fruit. You want to shoot for something that everyone can relate to, and that's why there is so much information flying around about the weather, the traffic, the latest viral video, and pop culture events.

However, author Laurie Helgoe put it best by stating, "We hate small talk because we hate the barrier it creates between people." Small talk allows us to have entire conversations where people speak a lot without saying anything. It just serves to fill the silence and it's how we go through the motions of social courtesy.

When small talk is left unattended and to its own devices, it usually degenerates into empty babble like the weather. Small talk becomes just that: small. It is shallow, superficial chatter and a waste of the precious social battery. This is draining for no purpose or rhyme or reason.

It doesn't have to be. Instead of dancing from shallow topic to shallow topic as you're accustomed to, just bypass it. Skip it and go straight to what's important or interesting to you. Deal with small talk by opting out of it from the start.

Instead of asking about the weather, ask how someone feels about the pending political situation. Instead of asking about the traffic, ask about someone's worldview in relation to their occupation. Instead of asking about how someone's weekend was, ask someone what their most embarrassing moment was. These questions don't break the ice—they skip that part of the conversation because it doesn't need to exist. There don't need to be courtesy questions about someone's background before diving into what they actually think and feel.

To deal best with small talk, avoid it completely and dive into meaningful topics and questions. If you are courteous and seem genuinely curious and nonjudgmental, the only boundaries you will be violating are in your own head. To continue with this trend, make it your goal to go *deep*. The problem with wide-ranging and expansive discussions is they are necessarily shallow. In practical terms, this means to stay on only a few topics at a time and go deeper within them. Narrow your field of inquiry and aim for an inch wide and a mile deep.

Key phrases:

1. Why?
2. Tell me more about that.
3. What was the thinking/motivation/intention behind that?
4. That reminds me of a time in my life...
5. How did that impact your life?
6. Can you elaborate more on that?
7. Tell me the origin of that story!
8. How did that make you feel?

See how you're going beyond the regular *who, what, when, where,* and *why*? You're focusing on the emotions that people feel and the consequences of the actions in their lives. At least your interactions will hold greater value to you than simply draining your social energy.

There is always some resistance to this proposition. It feels *invasive* and like you are verging into topics that are *inappropriate*. But that's all arbitrary. Instead, ask yourself what topics you discuss with your friends and how you engage with them. Think back to the last few conversations you had with a close friend. Now contrast that with a conversation you might have with a stranger you meet at a networking event.

Consider that, when you don't speak personally and to what feels *inappropriate* with strangers, you are unintentionally holding them at arm's length and making sure they remain strangers. People tend to follow the tone others set, so if you treat them with familiarity and rapport, that's how they will treat you.

Takeaways:

- This chapter is what you might deem the advice section of the book. It's all about how introverts can better socialize within the confines of what holds them back—their social batteries.
- Introverts must learn to categorize and plan their interactions. They can

generally create four categories for interactions based on how many hours they can withstand. They can also begin to plan around energy expenditure rather than how much time is free. This helps keep them out of harm's way instead of unintentionally stressing themselves out. The common thread behind those tactics is to find predictability and use it to your advantage.

- When introverts reach an interaction, there are a few ways to help them last longer and generally be more social. First, become a question master and draw information out of others rather than generating it yourself. You can do this effectively by mixing broad and specific questions to avoid sounding like an interviewer. Second, take the step of completely bypassing what we would call small talk. No one enjoys it, so you'll be doing everyone a favor by skipping it and heading directly for personal topics. The point here is to make sure that your energy expenditure isn't wasted on simply discussing the weather or the traffic.

Summary Guide

Chapter 1. The Personality Spectrum

- The personality spectrum has been defined in many ways throughout history, but people have increasingly gravitated toward classifying themselves in terms of their capacity for social interaction and how important a person's internal or external world was. It was later refined to understand that introverts are depleted by social interaction, while extroverts are recharged by it. This leads to opposite types of lifestyles, as you might suspect. There are a variety of misunderstandings associated with these labels, but keep in mind that this scale solely judges what makes people feel recharged—solitude or company.

- Even though Carl Jung defined these two terms and forever created a spectrum, he recognized that it was impossible for people to not be in the middle. These are called ambiverts, and the vast majority of us are ambiverts. We act according to social obligation, circumstance, and duty, which means you can't necessarily tell someone's temperament just by their actions alone. We might skew to one side or another and can further categorize ourselves with terms like extroverted introvert or introverted extrovert. This still means we are in the middle in terms of our social battery, capacity, and desire.

- A point of distinction must be made between introverts and highly sensitive people—HSPs. They may appear identical at first glance, but that's where the similarities end. The HSP is characterized by the acronym DOES, which stands for depth of processing, overstimulation, emotional reactivity, and sensing the subtle. This all amounts to HSPs wearing a proverbial hearing aid turned up to the max when none is needed. They are *sensitive*, and this merely overlaps with social capacity and recharging.

Chapter 2. Inside-Out

- This chapter is a look at the different biological differences that place people where they are on the introvert/extrovert spectrum. No matter what someone's behavior is, it will always start from a baseline that their biology has set.

- The first biological difference is that introverts have denser brain matter in the prefrontal cortex, which is where analysis, ruminating, decision-making, and planning take place. In fact, it's where most stereotypical introverted behaviors take place. It also explains why introverts are said to be focused more on their internal worlds versus the external world—because they are literally stuck in their thoughts more than extroverts. To support this, extroverts were shown to have increased blood flow to areas involved in sensory processing, which allows them to focus on their external world.

- Dopamine and acetylcholine are at the heart of another difference in how introverts and extroverts process external stimuli. Extroverts have blunted dopamine receptors, so they need more stimulation to feel pleasure. Introverts have heightened dopamine receptors, so they feel overwhelmed more easily. This leads them to seek out activities and behaviors that generate acetylcholine, which creates feelings of tranquility and calm.

- The final major biological difference is the level of background noise that is inside the introvert's or extrovert's mind. To put it plainly, introverts have perpetual static and chatter in their mind, which makes them more liable to overwhelm, analysis, rumination, and retreating to solitude. Hans Eysenck proved a corollary of this with his lemon juice test, in which he found that introverts were generally easier to arouse and become alert.

- All of these differences make it seem like introverts are somewhat less predisposed to survival than extroverts. But the opposite is true; zoological studies have found that there are generally two groups in a society, rovers and sitters, and both are needed because they complement each other. Rovers are extroverts—thrill-seekers and out and about. Sitters are introverts—planners, analyzers, and operating in the background. That is to say, introverts keep themselves and the people around them safer than they might be otherwise.

Chapter 3. The Pursuit of Happiness

- Happiness—it is different for everyone, and the only thing we know is that we want it. That, or we want to avoid unhappiness; either will suffice most of the time. There is a marked difference in happiness levels between introverts (sadder) and extroverts (happier). You might consider two paths: (1) extroverts have a greater probability of being exposed to happiness-inducing events or

(2) extrovert tendencies stemming from biological differences cause extroverts to evaluate their lives in more positive ways.

- With the difference in happiness, a natural question becomes whether introverts can change their personalities to be more extroverted and thus happier. The answer? Yes. If people can overcome phobias and traumatic brain injuries such as a stroke, they can also create neural change in personalities. But it takes commitment, a plan, and strong motivation like any change.

- Aging also changes the personality— four out of the five big five personality traits were found to decrease with age, though not before increasing for a spell during young adulthood.

Chapter 4. The Science of Introversion

- Though it is the topic of this book, this chapter in particular presents introverts from a broad perspective. Through the lens of the most recent research, we learn quite a bit more about introverts than the fact that their social batteries are king.

- Introverts are more judgmental than extroverts because of how much they live inside their heads and think. Naturally, they think everyone else should act like this when it's not true.

- Introverts should be wary of caffeine because it simulates the type of stimulation that can overwhelm a social battery.

- There are four different types of introverts: social, anxious, restrained, and thinking.

- Introverts and covert narcissists share many of the same traits, though they end up there through completely different means. But still, there might be an overlap between the two populations.

- Introverts have been shown to literally not be able to distinguish faces from flowers. This is a peek into how they perceive and value social situations.

- Introverts use more concrete, judgmental, and intentional language, while extroverts are slower to judge, more flexible, and more open to interpretation.

Chapter 5. Temperamental Relationships

- Interpersonal relationships are the root of why we discuss introversion and extroversion, for the most part. We want to understand ourselves and the people around us better to increase the happiness and fulfillment of everyone's lives. That's my optimistic interpretation, anyway. So what dynamics exist in the context of personality and temperament?
- What happens when an introvert and extrovert become partners? Compromise is paramount because what each partner values, the other expressly does not want. A key here is to focus on social hobbies—shared activities with a social aspect and an activity or interest-based aspect. However, it can also be said that these two personalities can complement and bring out the best in

each other, compensating for perceived shortcomings and allowing each partner to focus on what they do best. It all depends.

- The overall lower happiness levels experienced by introverts also carry over into relationships.

- When it comes to sex, extroverts definitively have more of it. Is this because they place themselves into more situations with the possibility for sex and the law of probability works in their favor or because they have higher libidos in general? Probably the former.

- Finally, when it comes to leadership, the answer again becomes "it depends." Extroverted leaders can excel when there is stress and in close quarters with employees, but introverts appear to be better at drawing more out of people and giving them the space they need to succeed. The best, as with everything, is probably a mixture, embodied by the ambivert—which we all are, anyway.

Chapter 6. Introvert Action Plan

- This chapter is what you might deem the advice section of the book. It's all about how introverts can better socialize within the confines of what holds them back—their social batteries.

- Introverts must learn to categorize and plan their interactions. They can generally create four categories for interactions based on how many hours they can withstand. They can also begin to plan around energy expenditure rather than how much time is free. This helps keep them out of harm's way instead of unintentionally stressing themselves out. The common thread behind those tactics is to find predictability and use it to your advantage.

- When introverts reach an interaction, there are a few ways to help them last longer and generally be more social. First, become a question master and draw information out of others rather than generating it yourself. You can do this effectively by mixing broad and specific questions to avoid sounding like an interviewer. Second, take the step of completely bypassing what we would call small talk. No one enjoys it, so you'll be doing everyone a favor by skipping it and heading directly for personal topics. The point here is to make sure that your energy expenditure isn't wasted on simply discussing the weather or the traffic.

Made in the USA
Coppell, TX
16 August 2020